THE PICTURE BOOK OF

HORSES

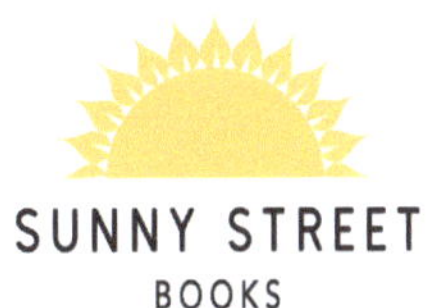

SUNNY STREET

BOOKS

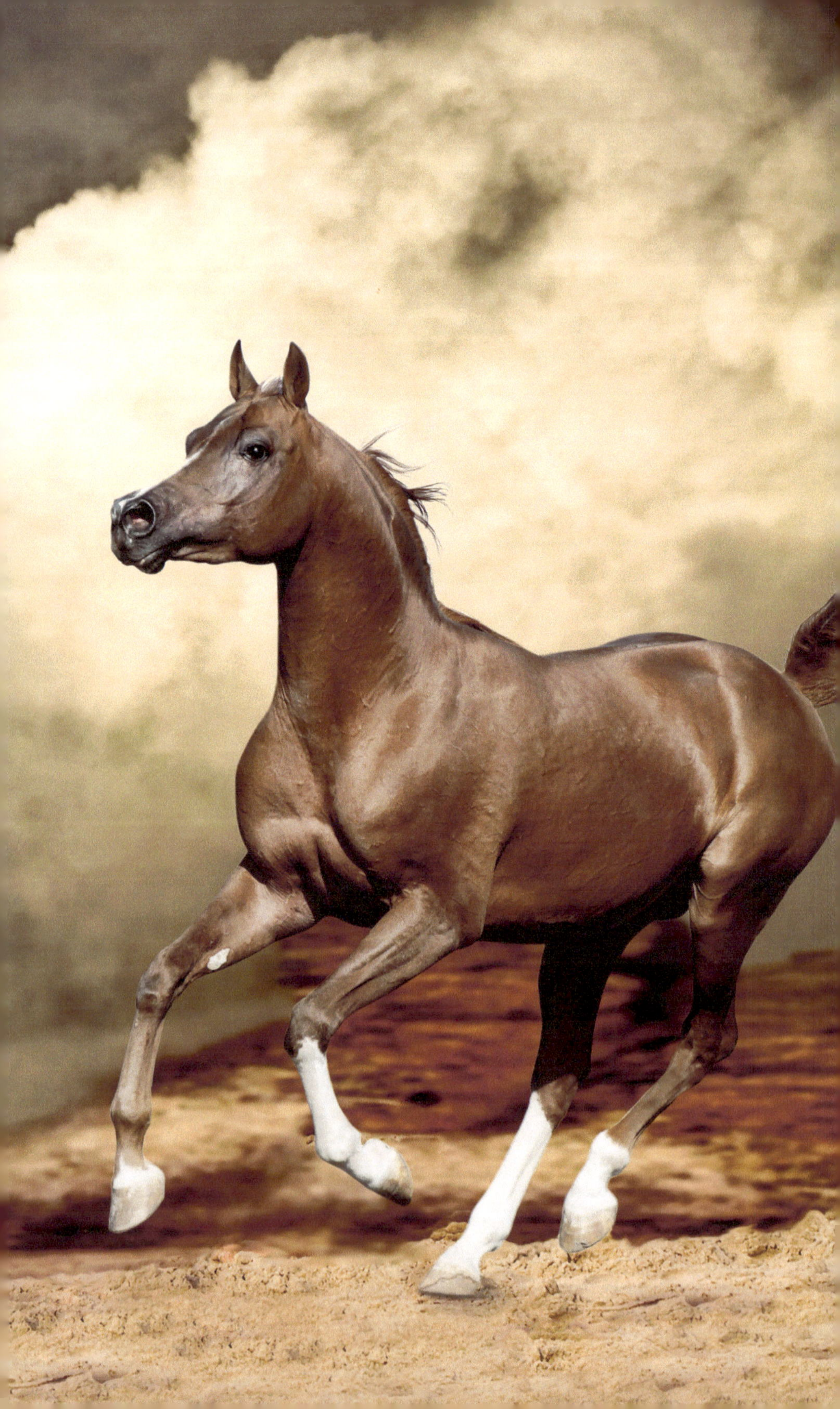

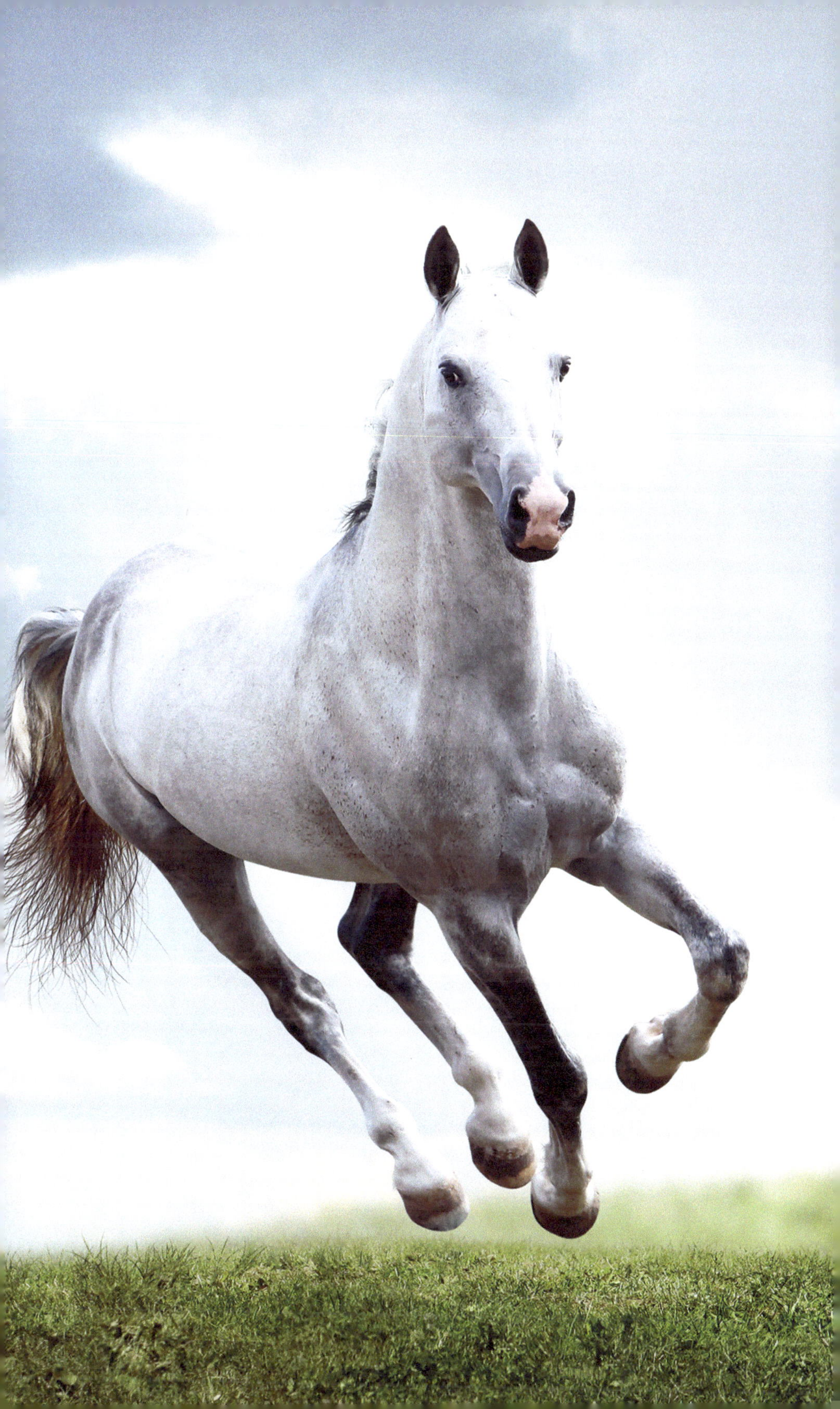

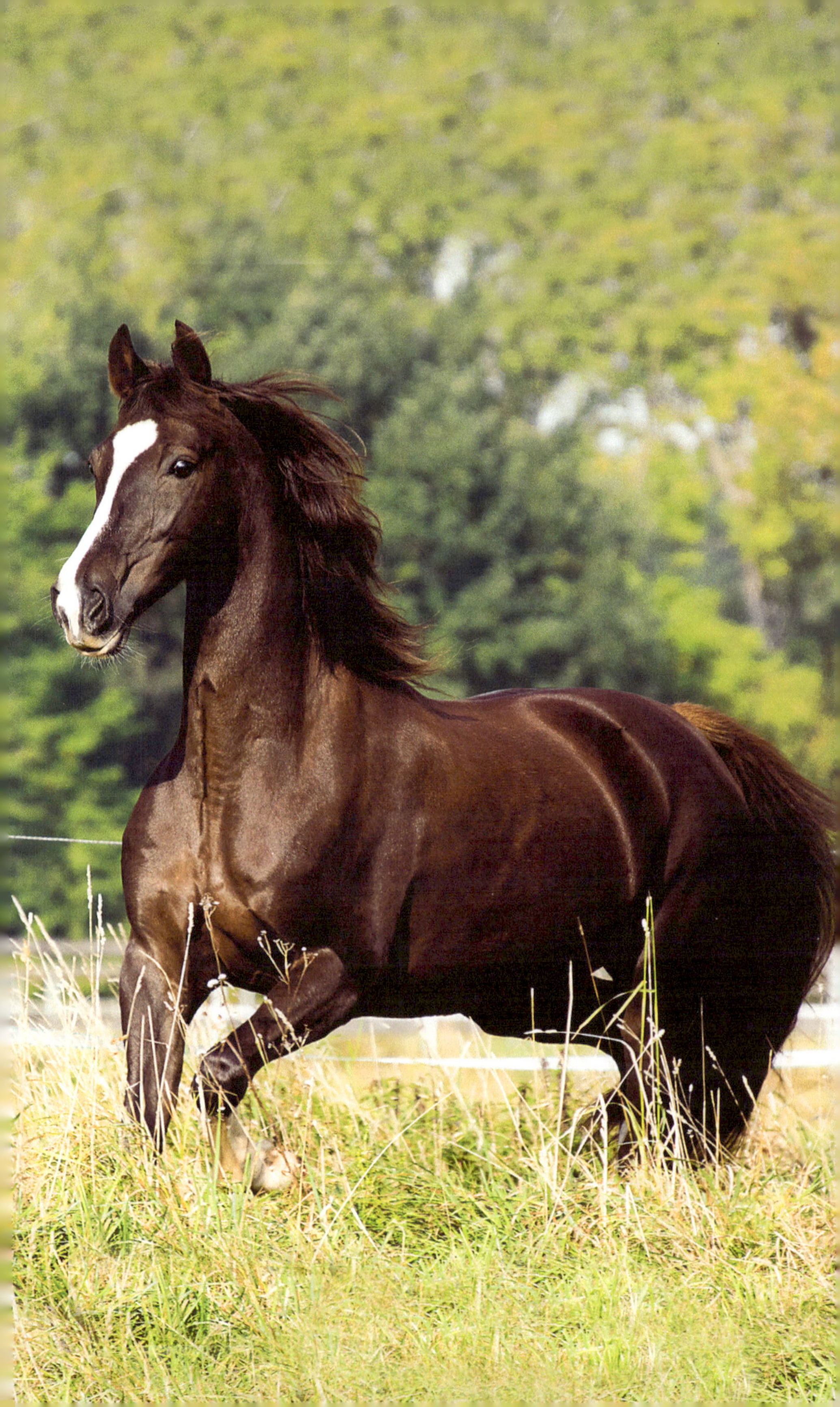

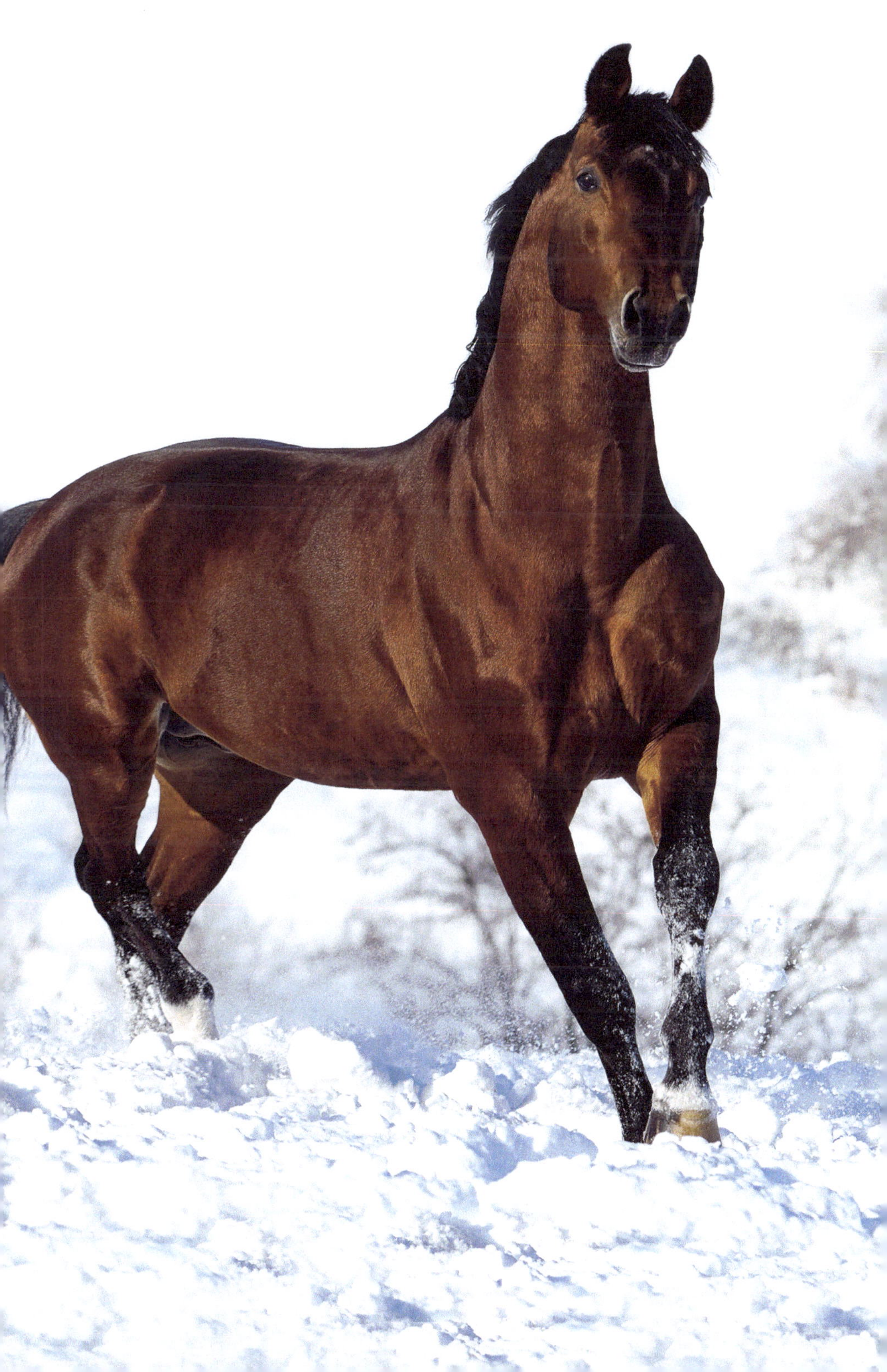

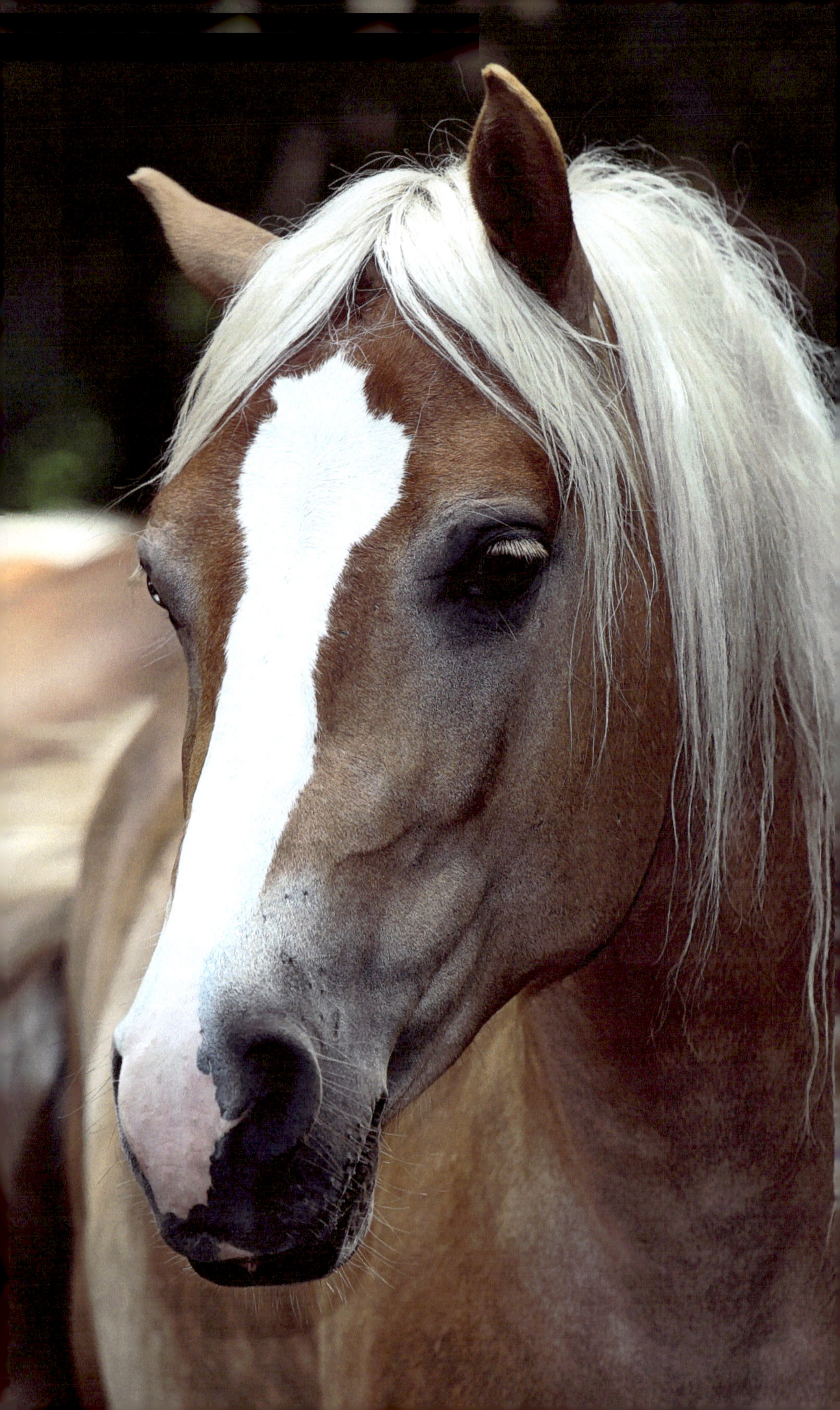

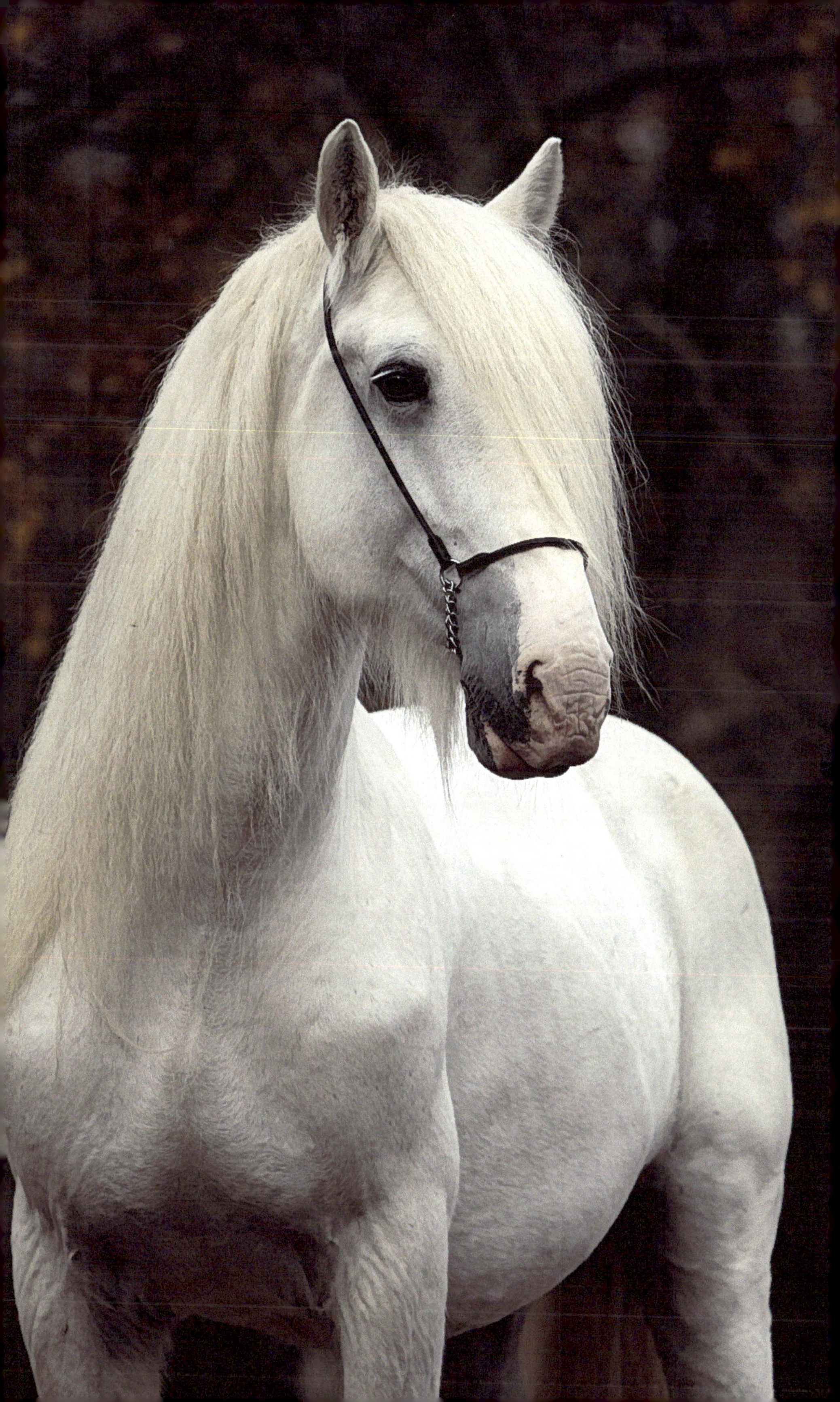

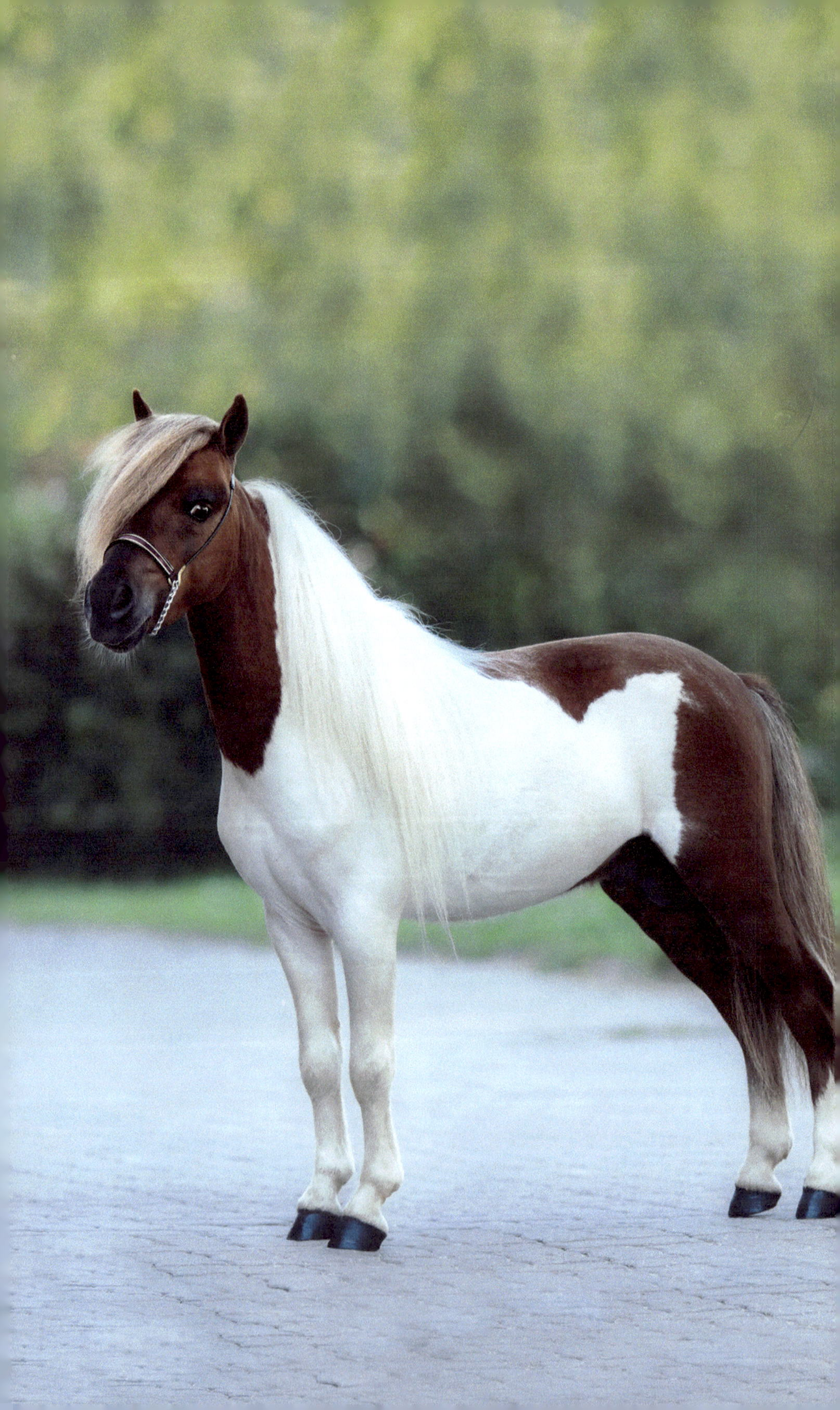

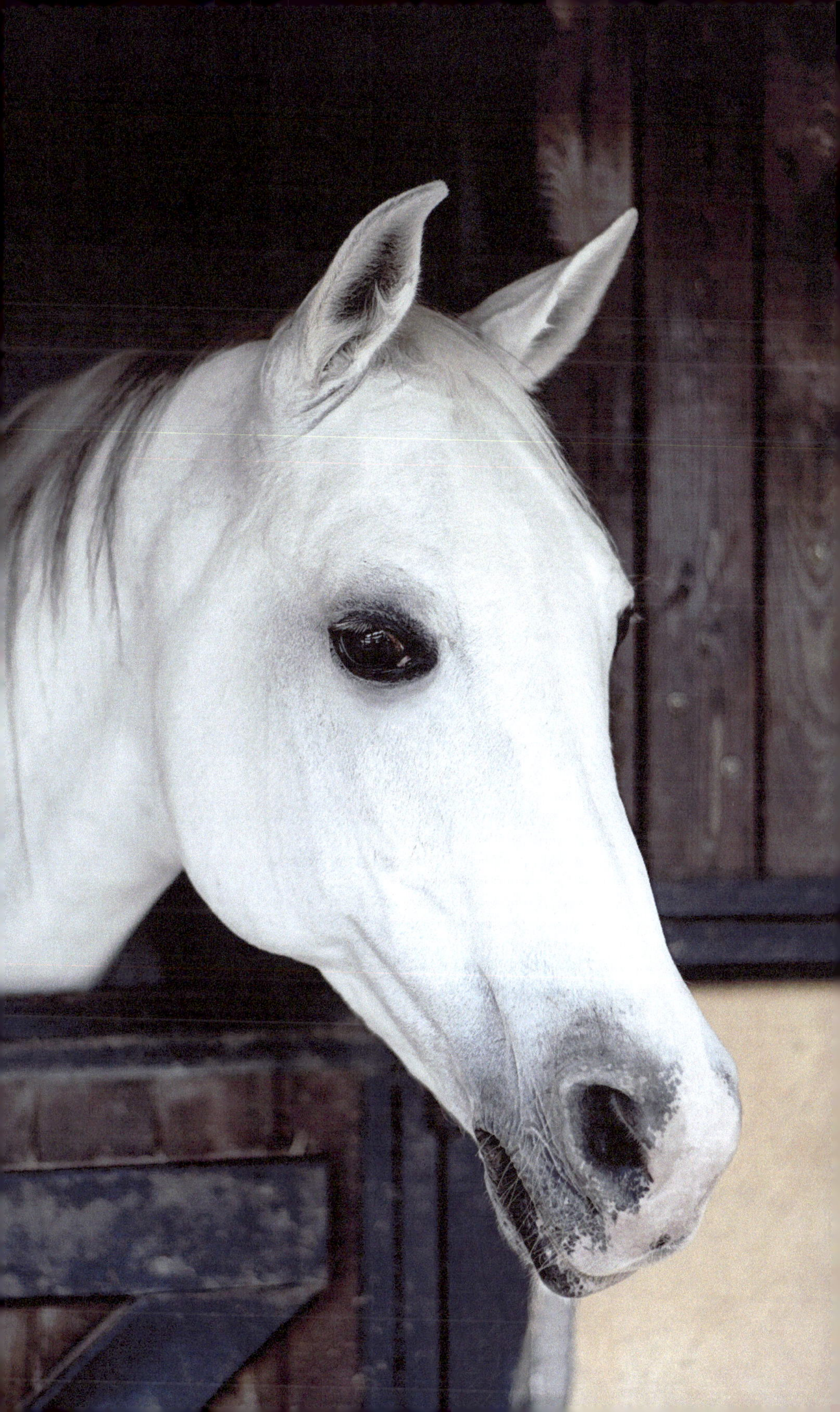

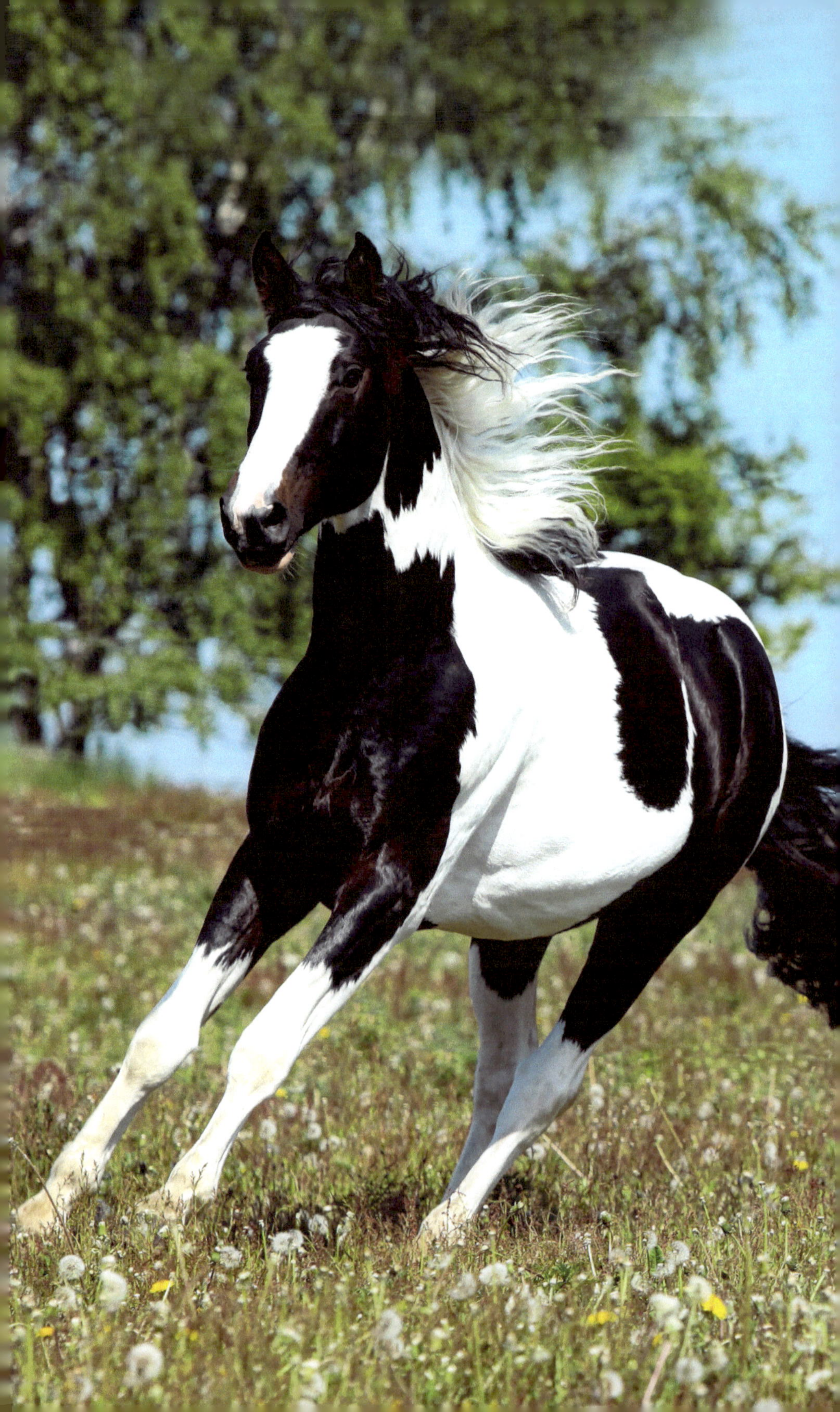

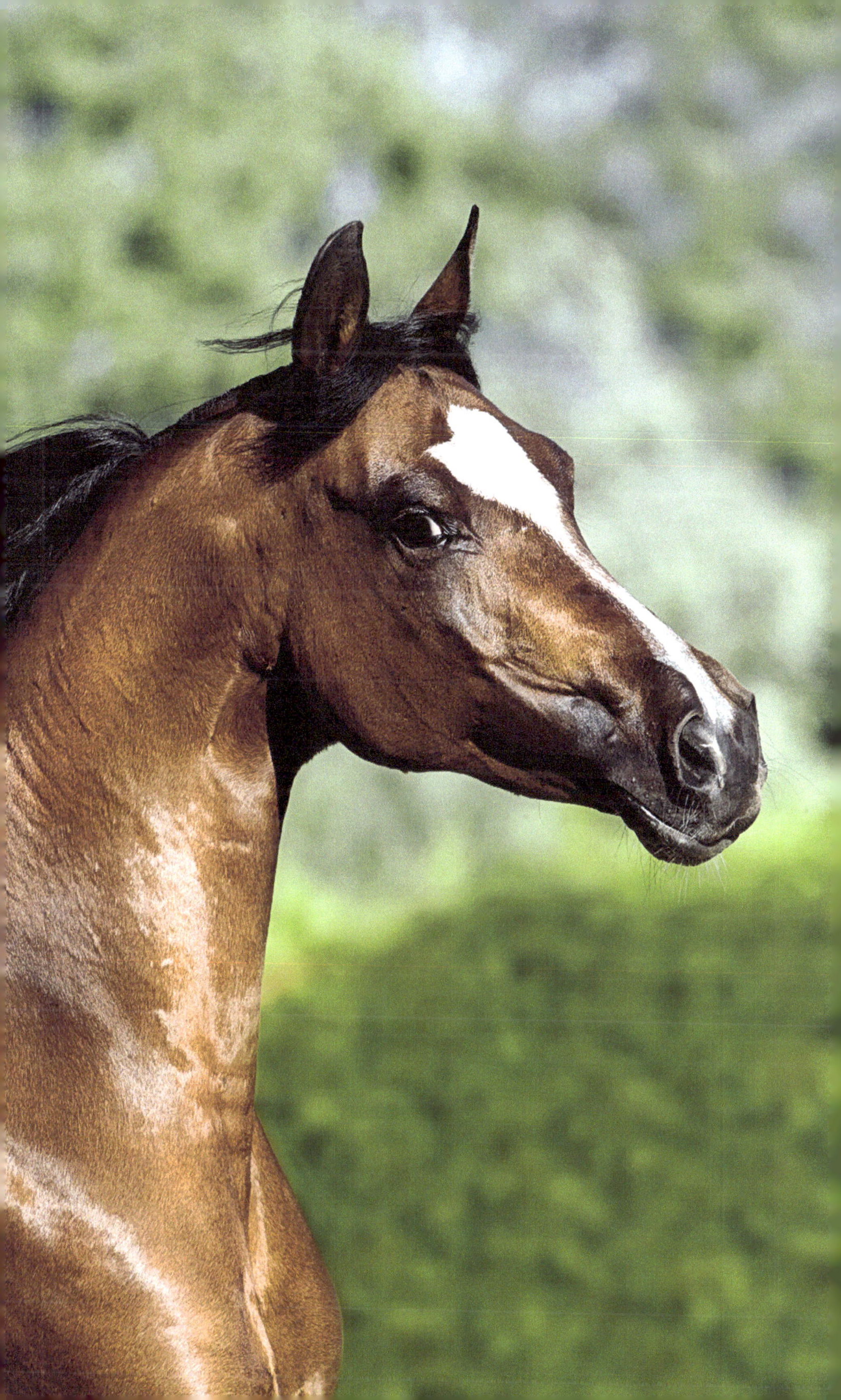

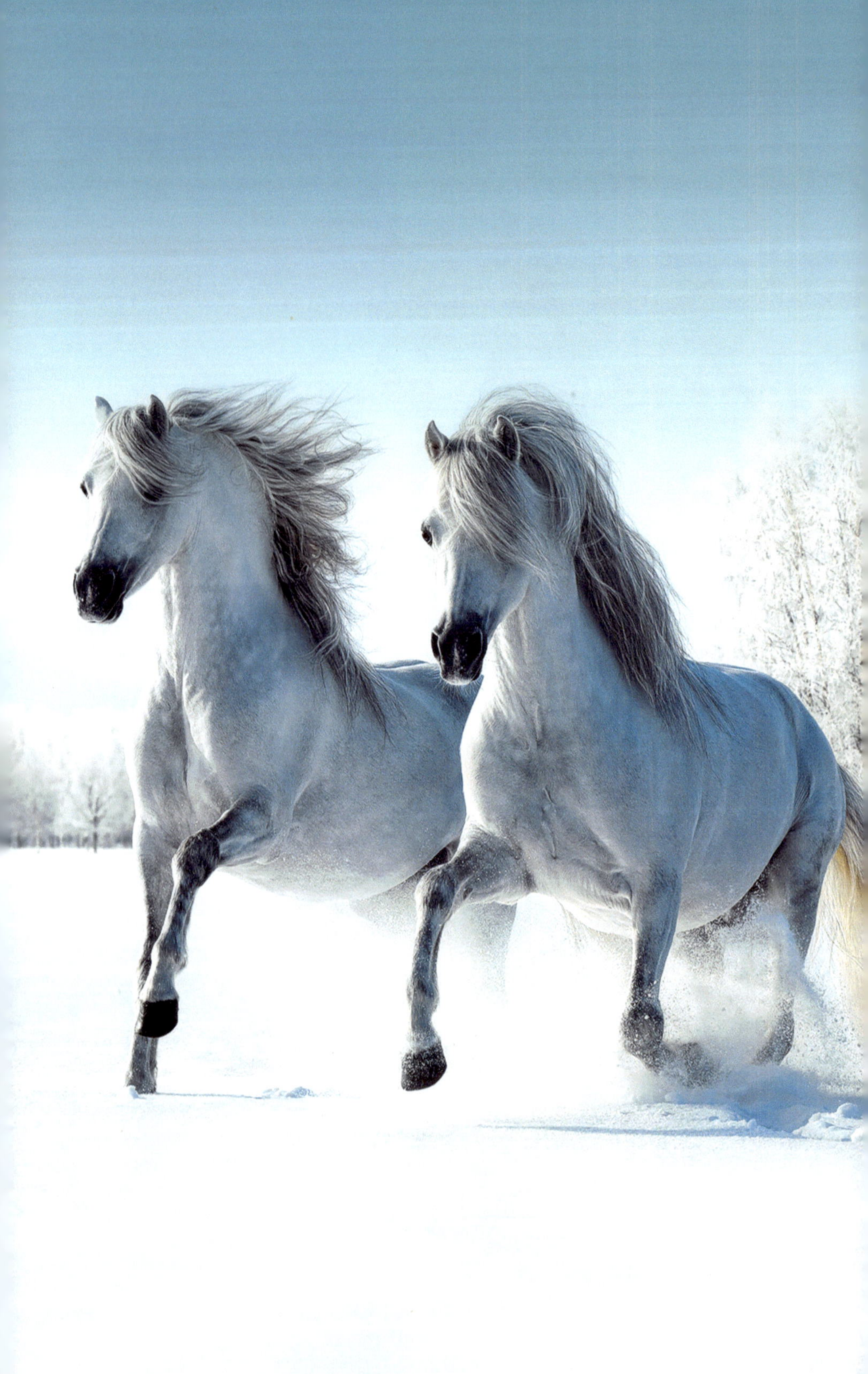

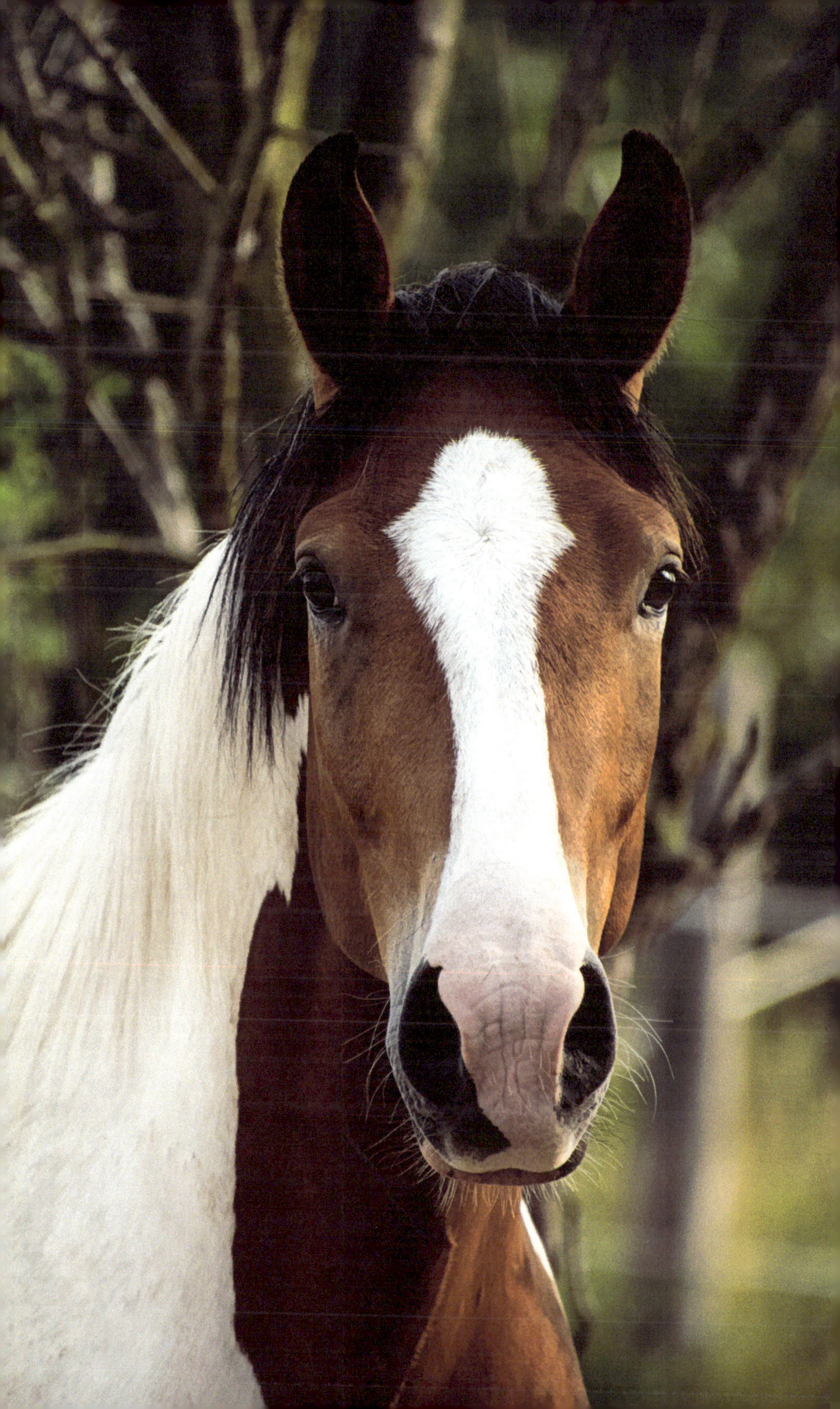

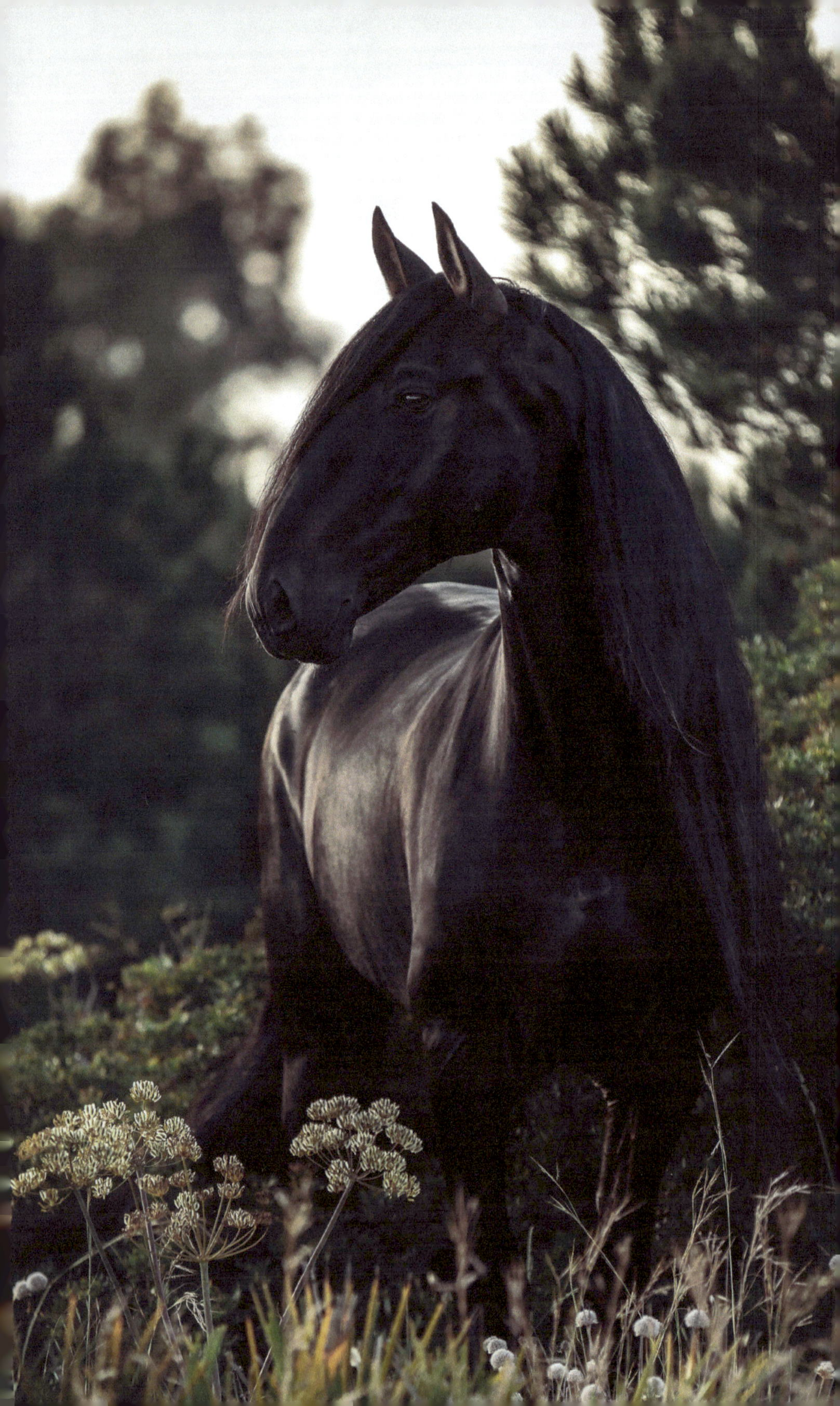

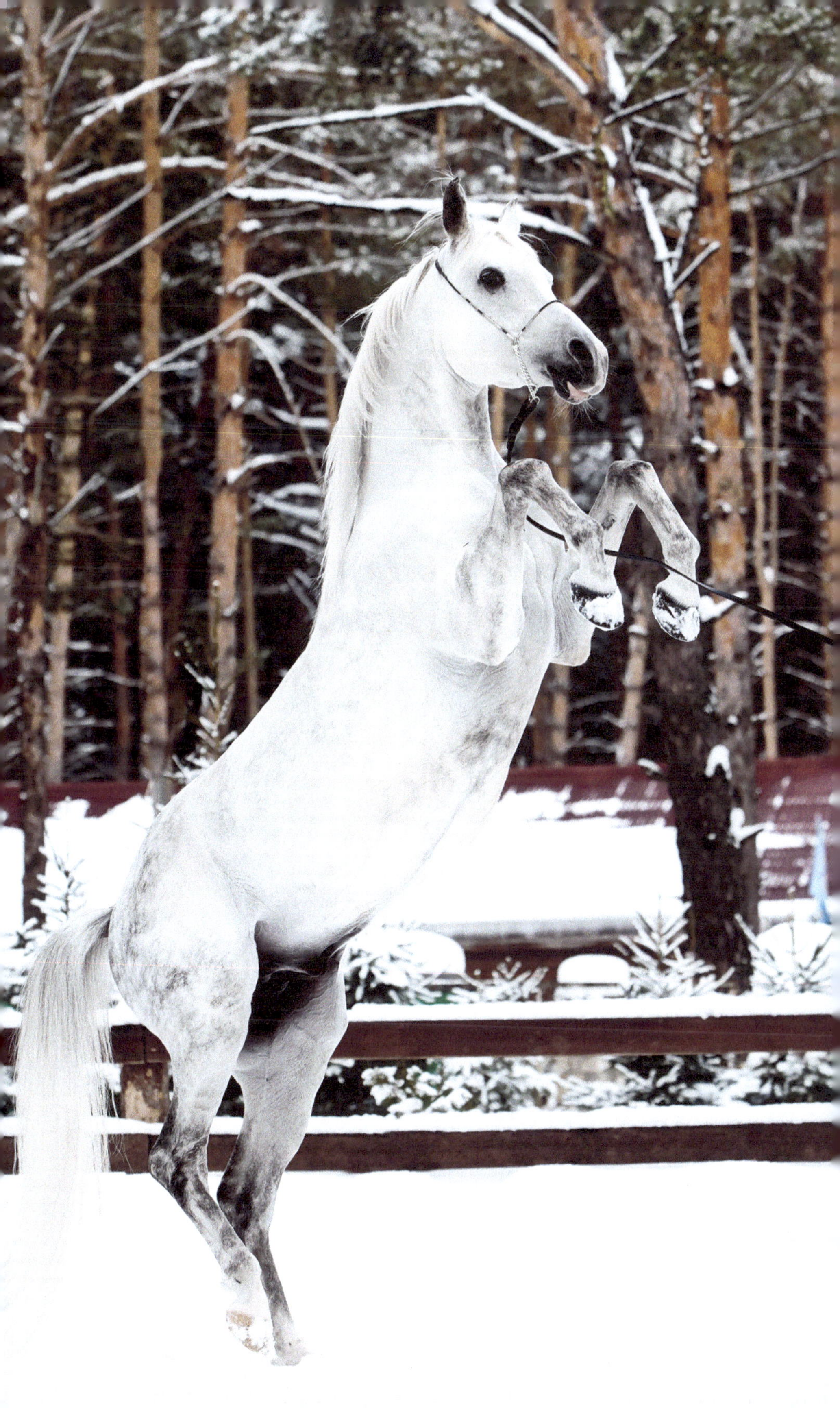

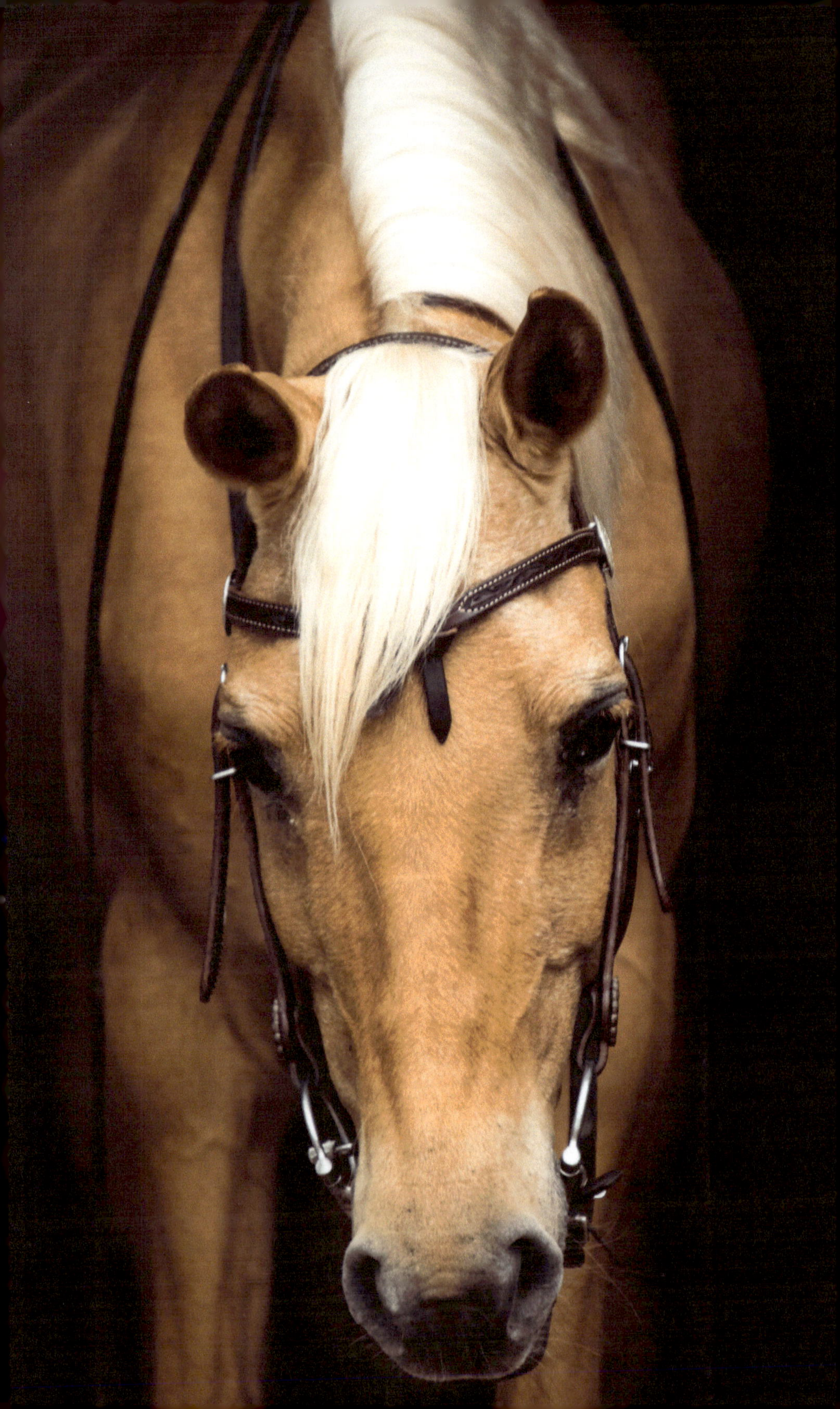

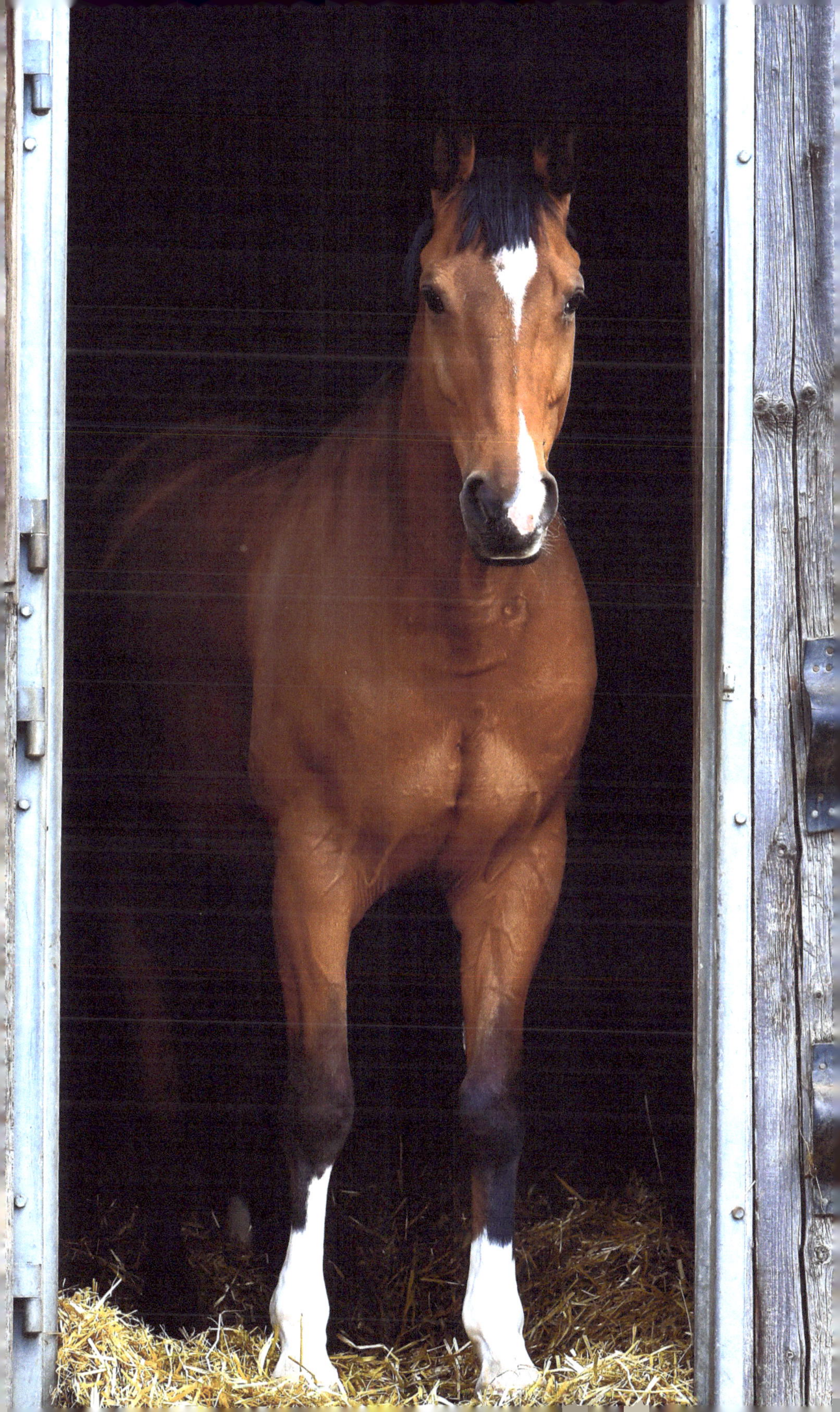

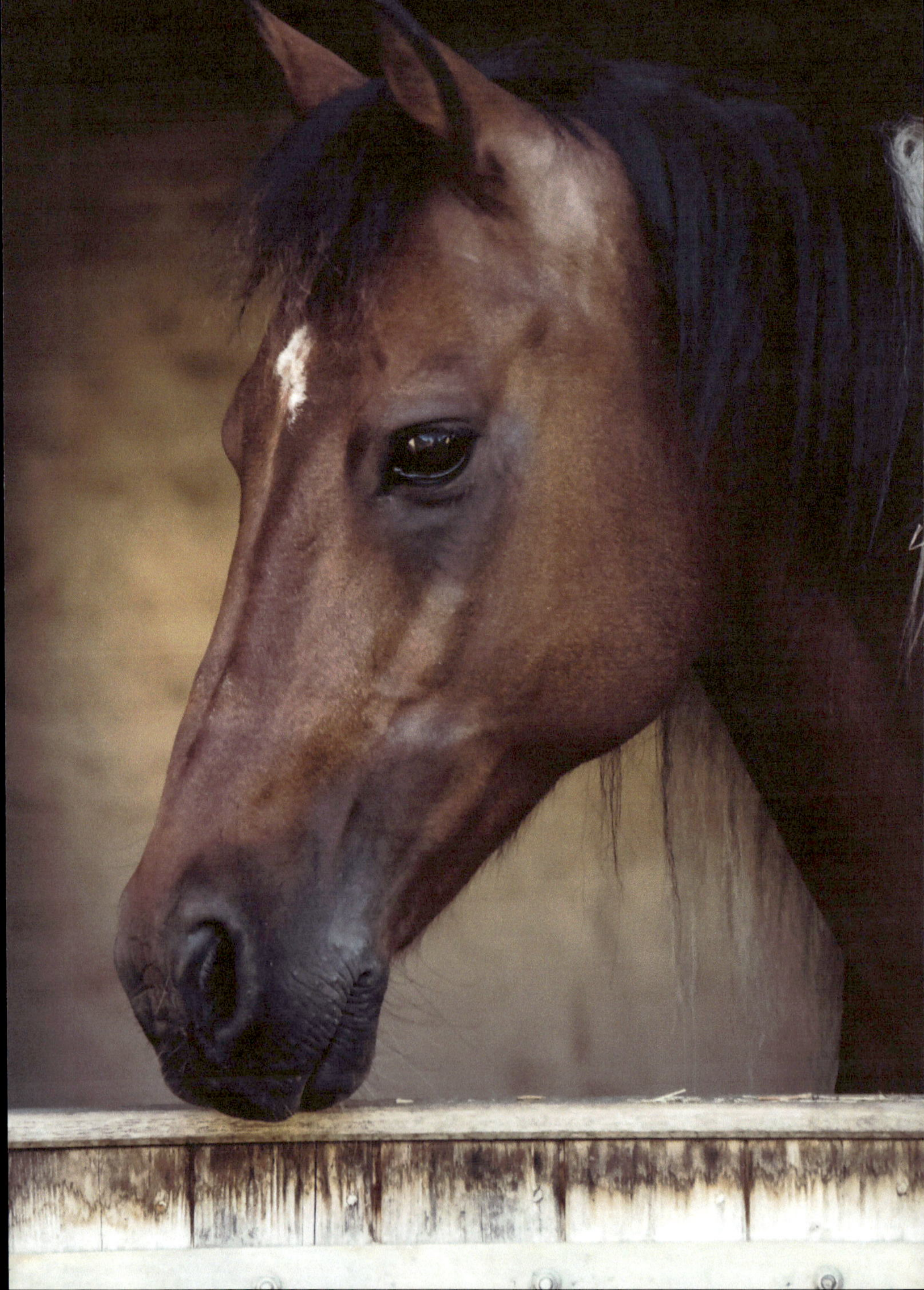

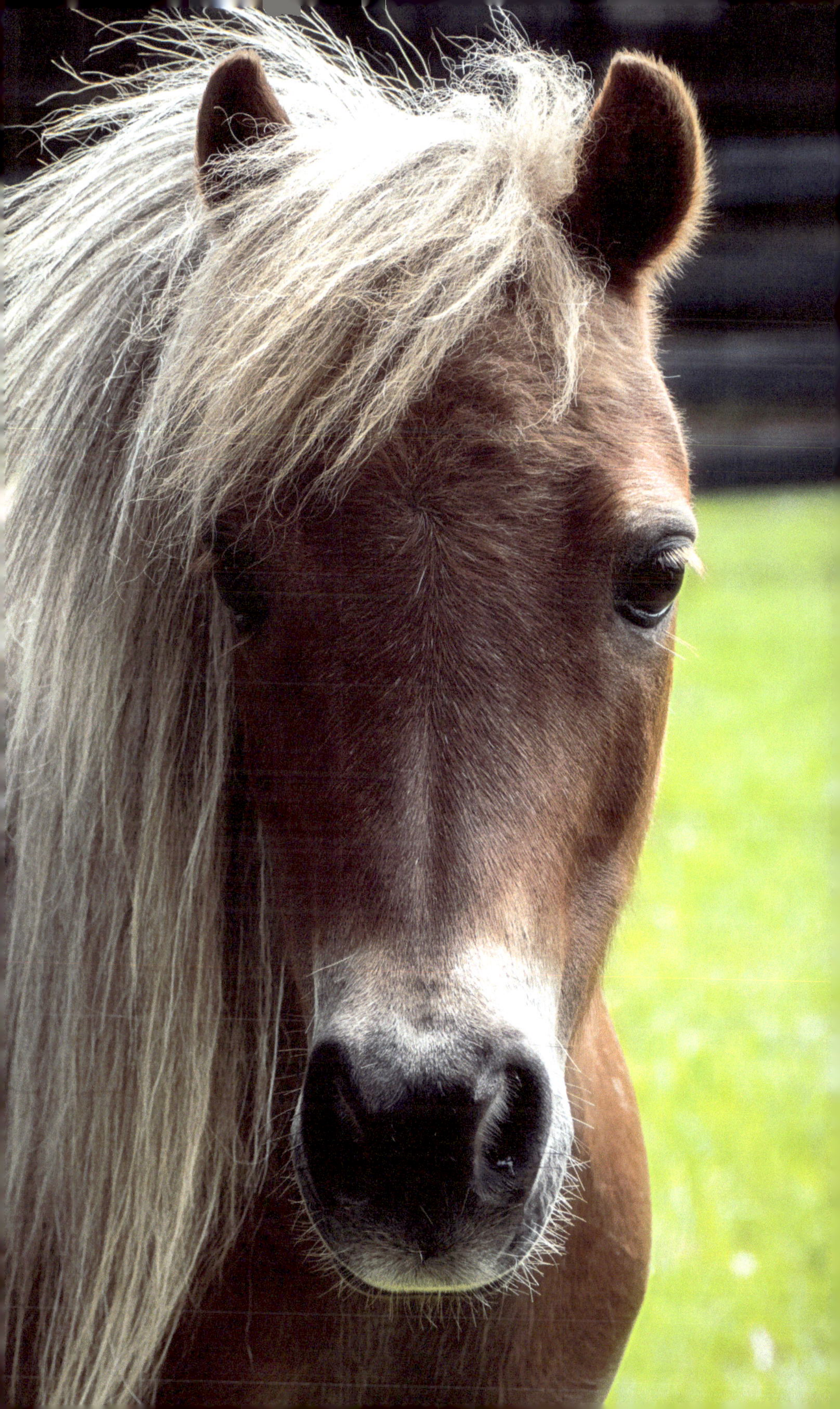

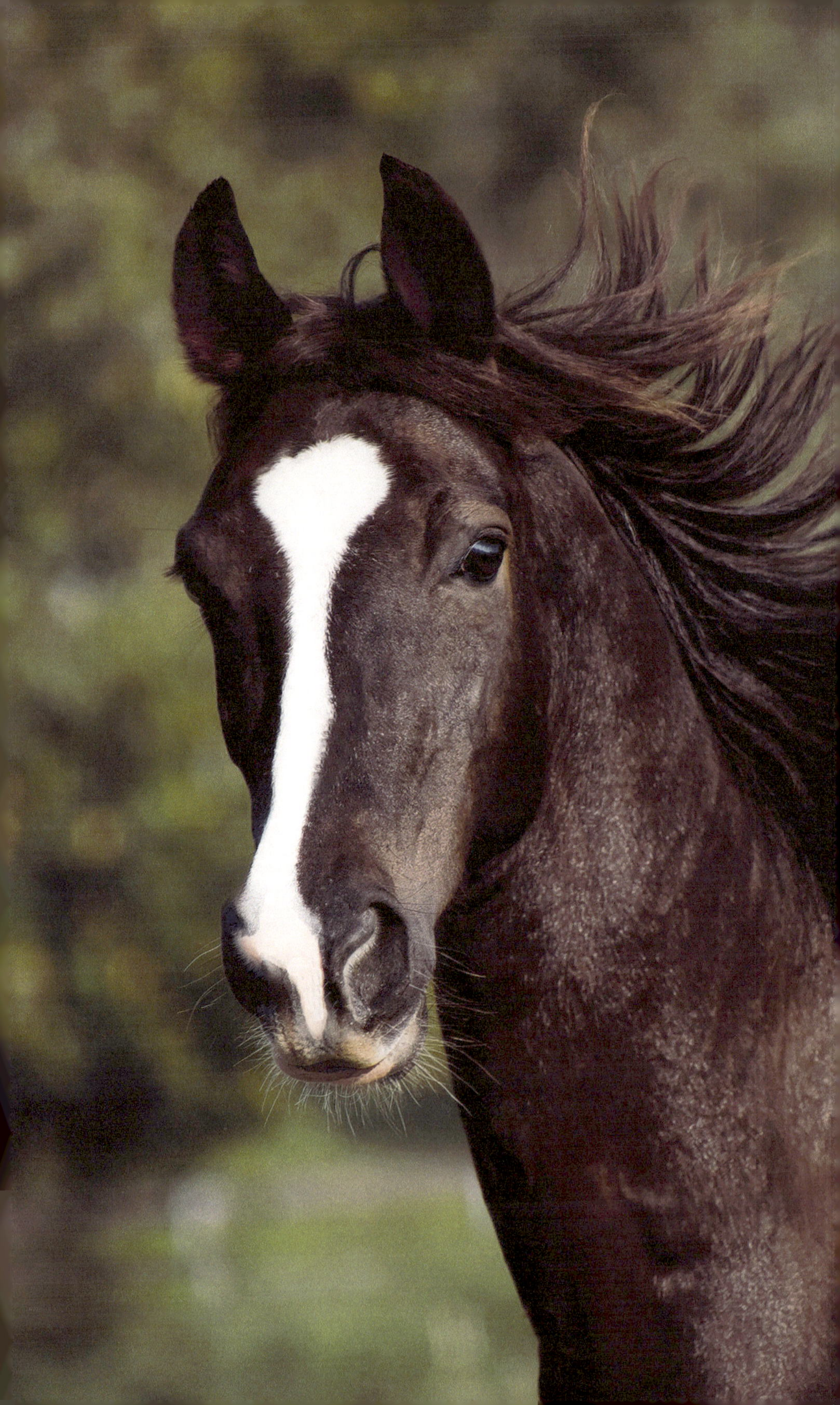

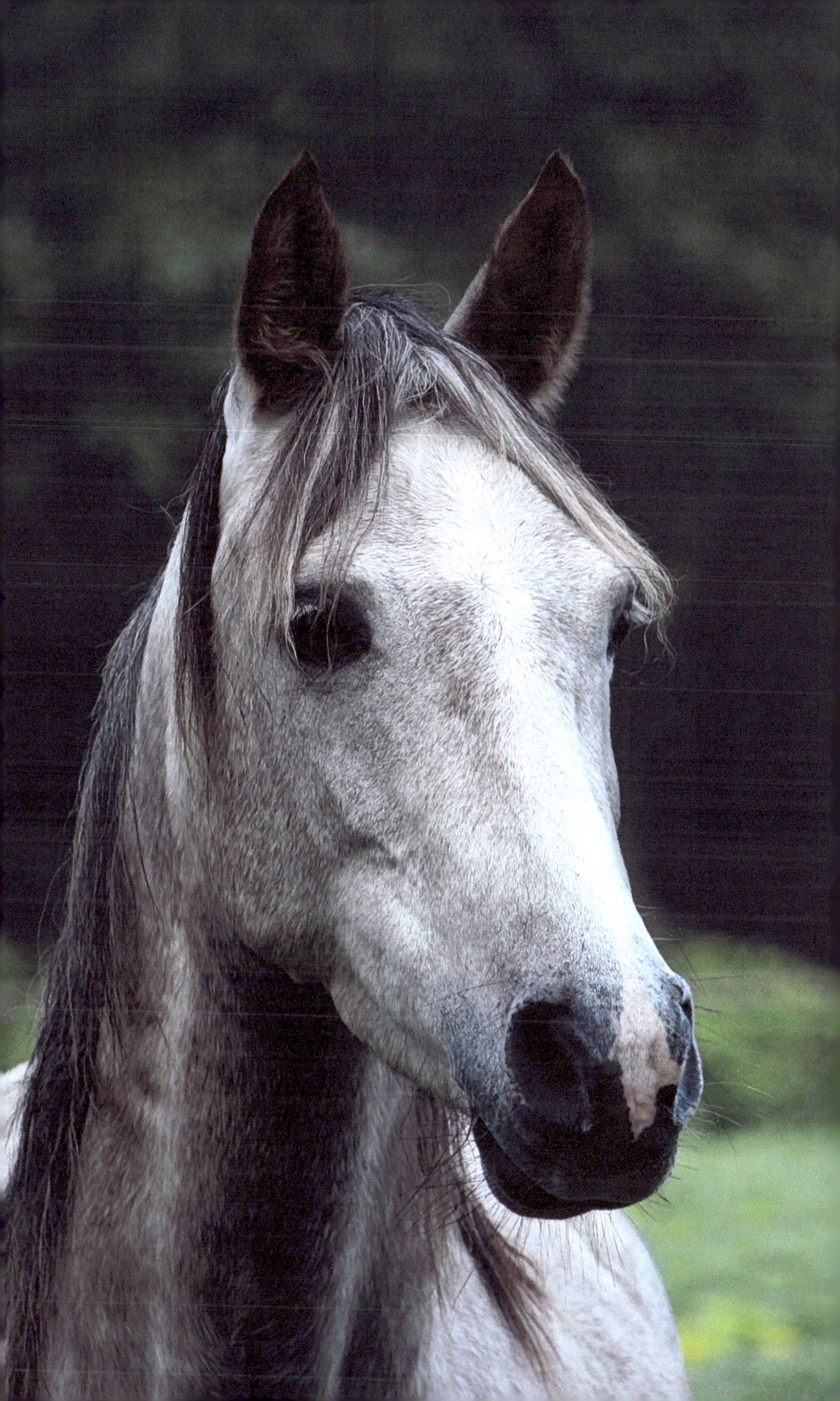

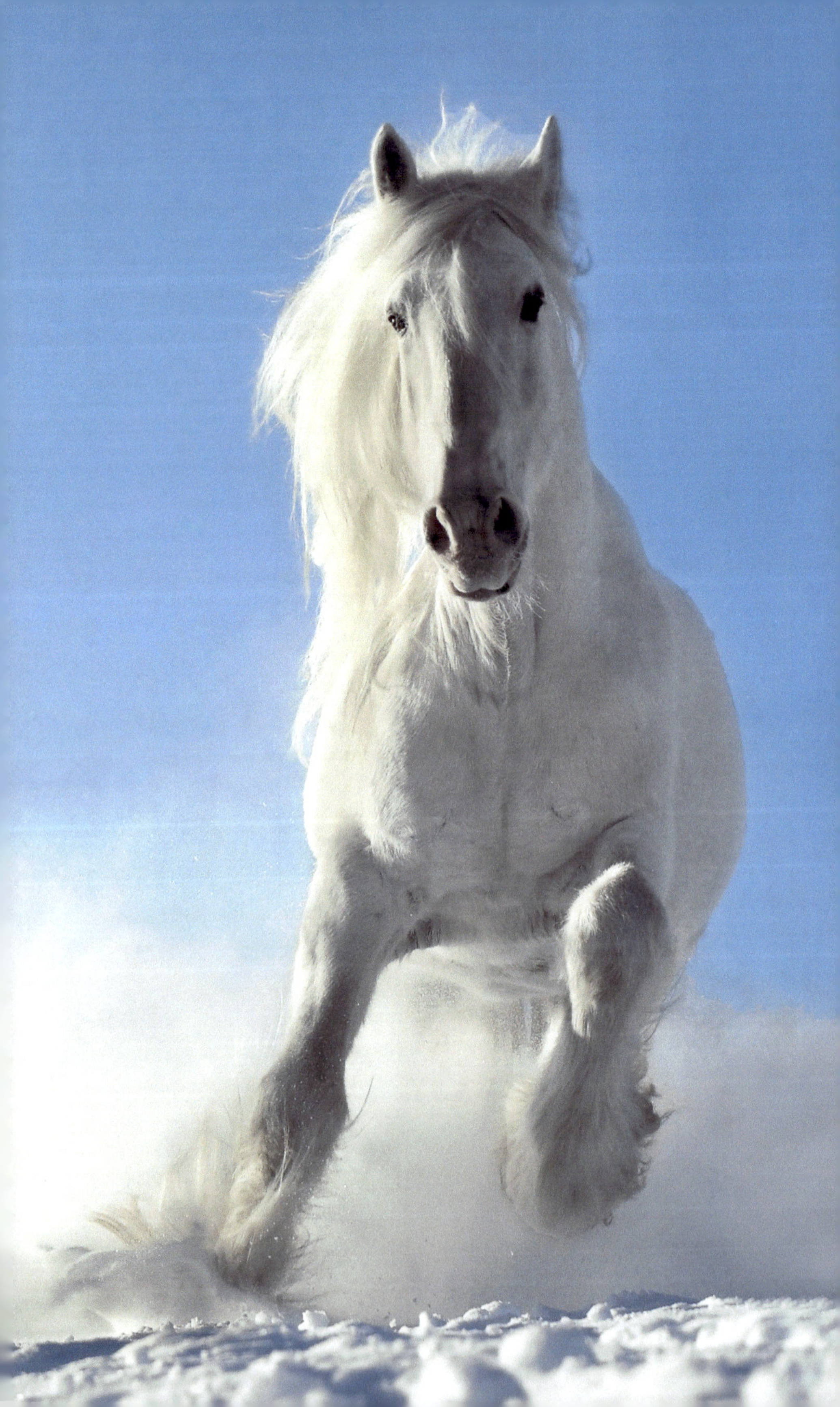

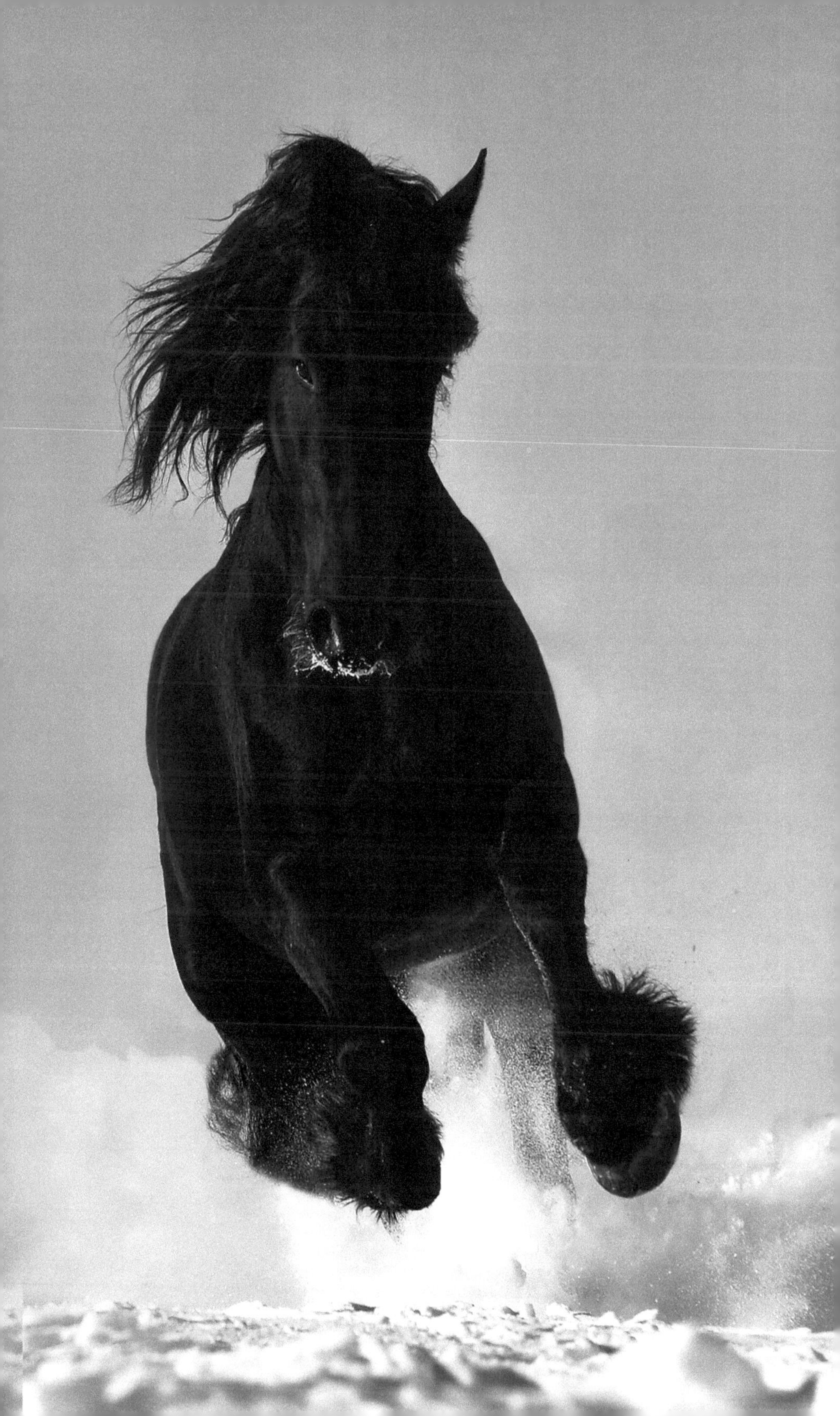

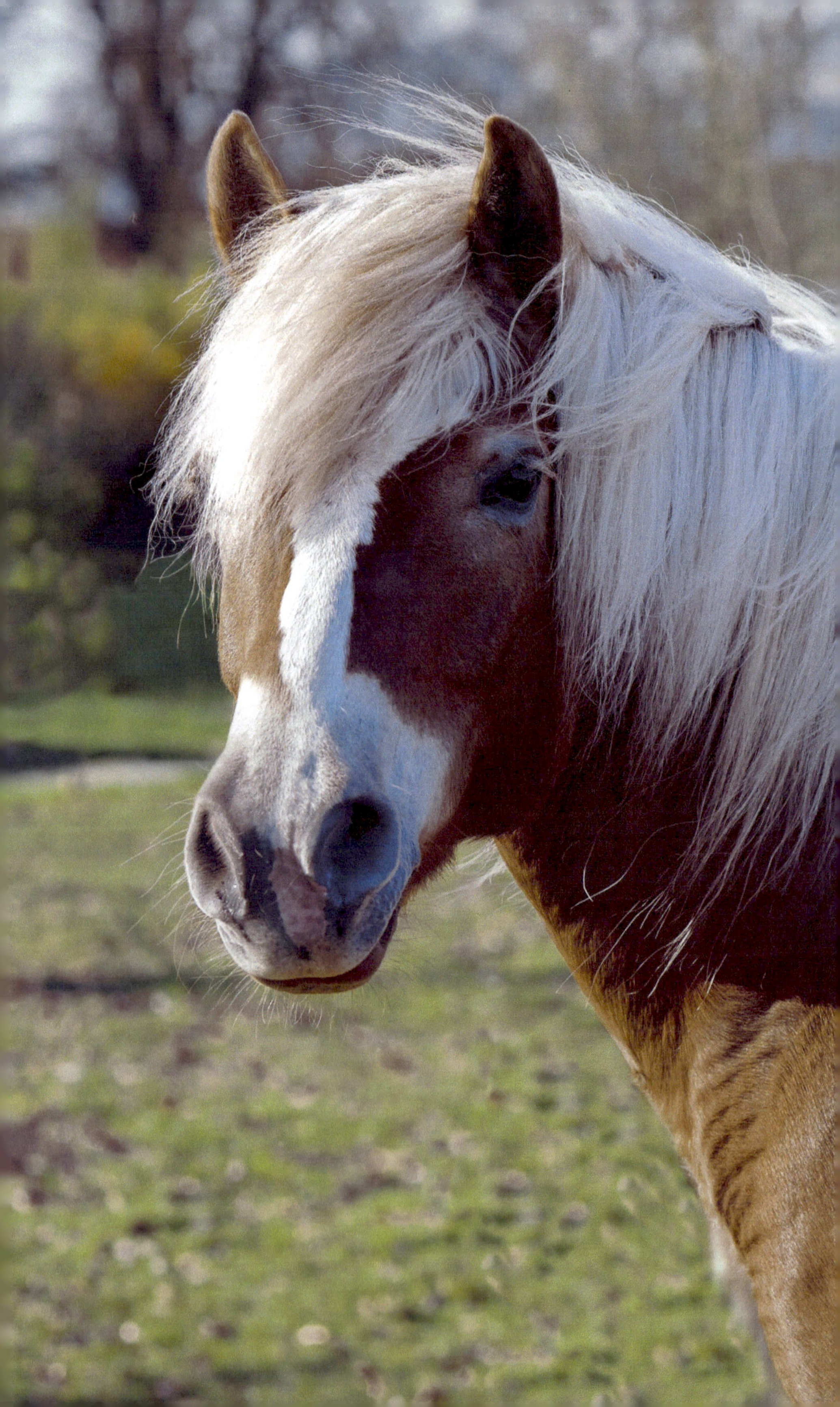

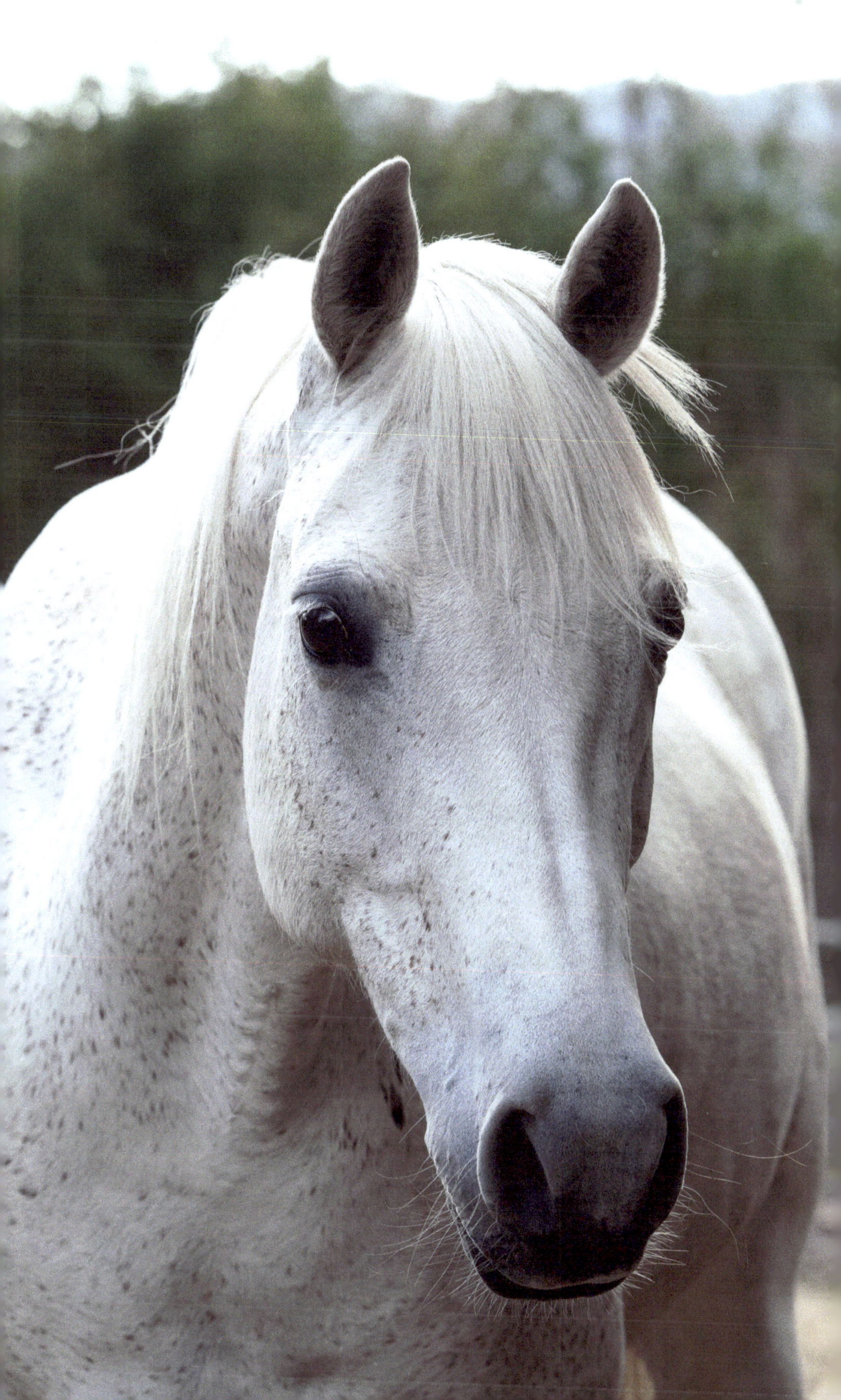

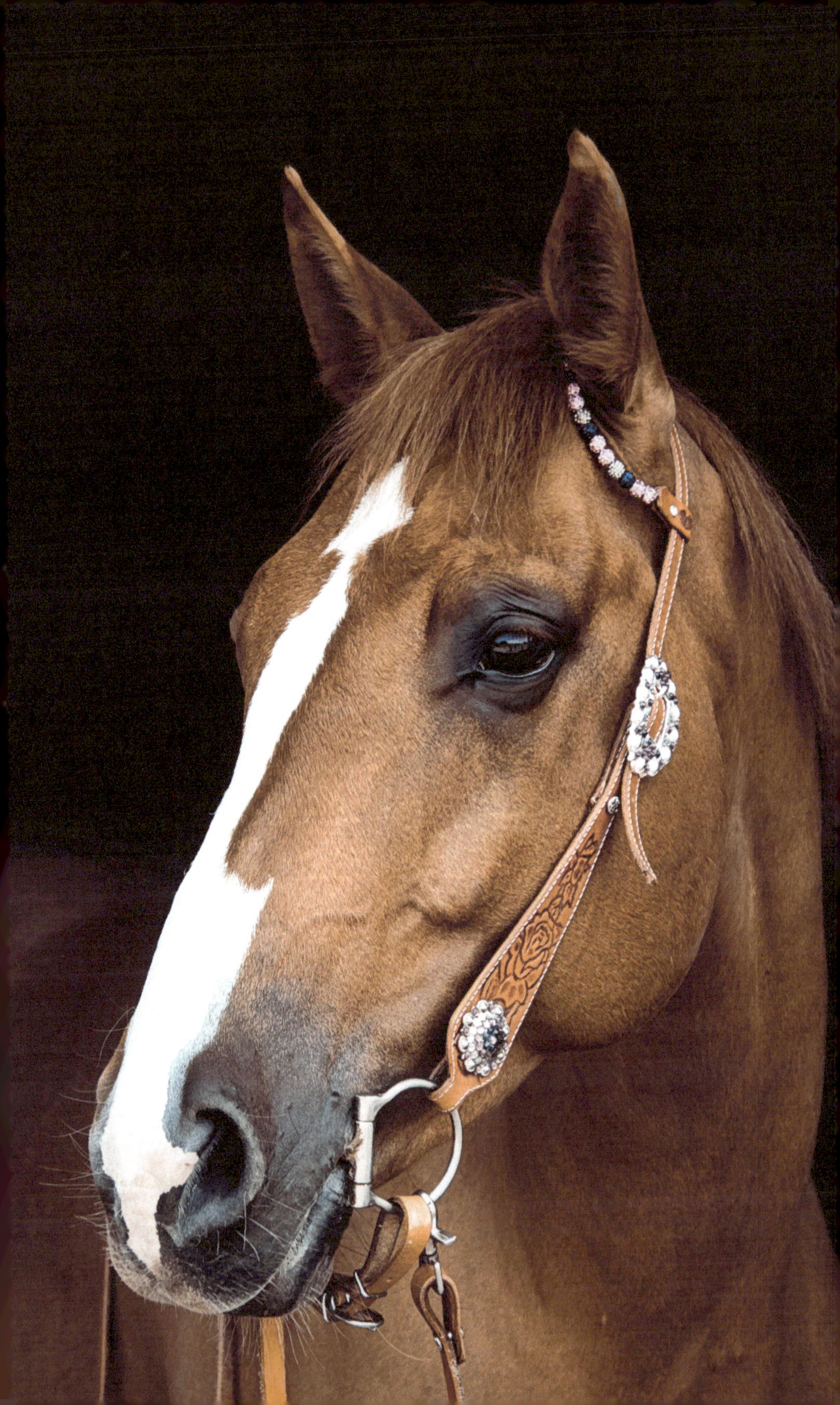

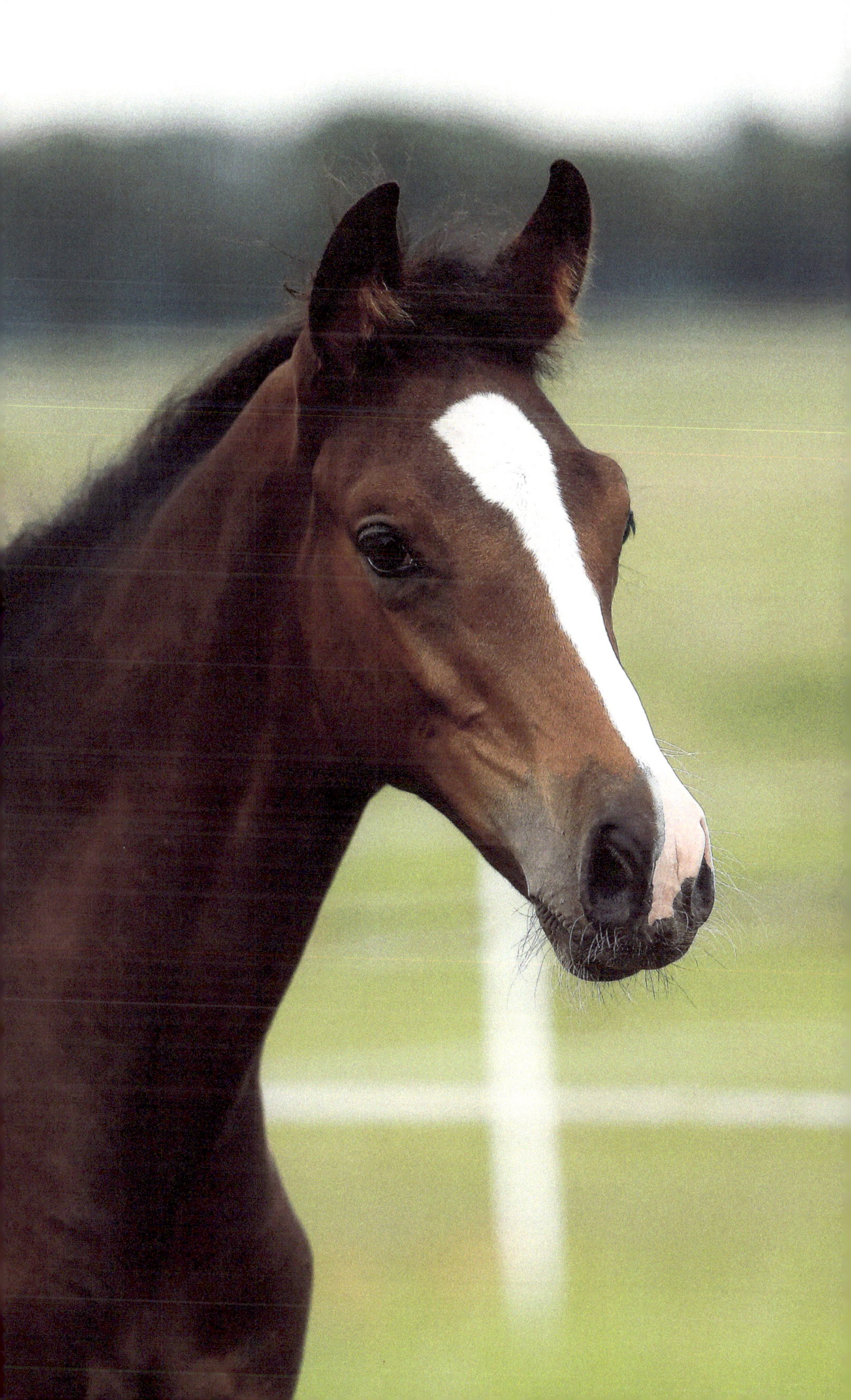

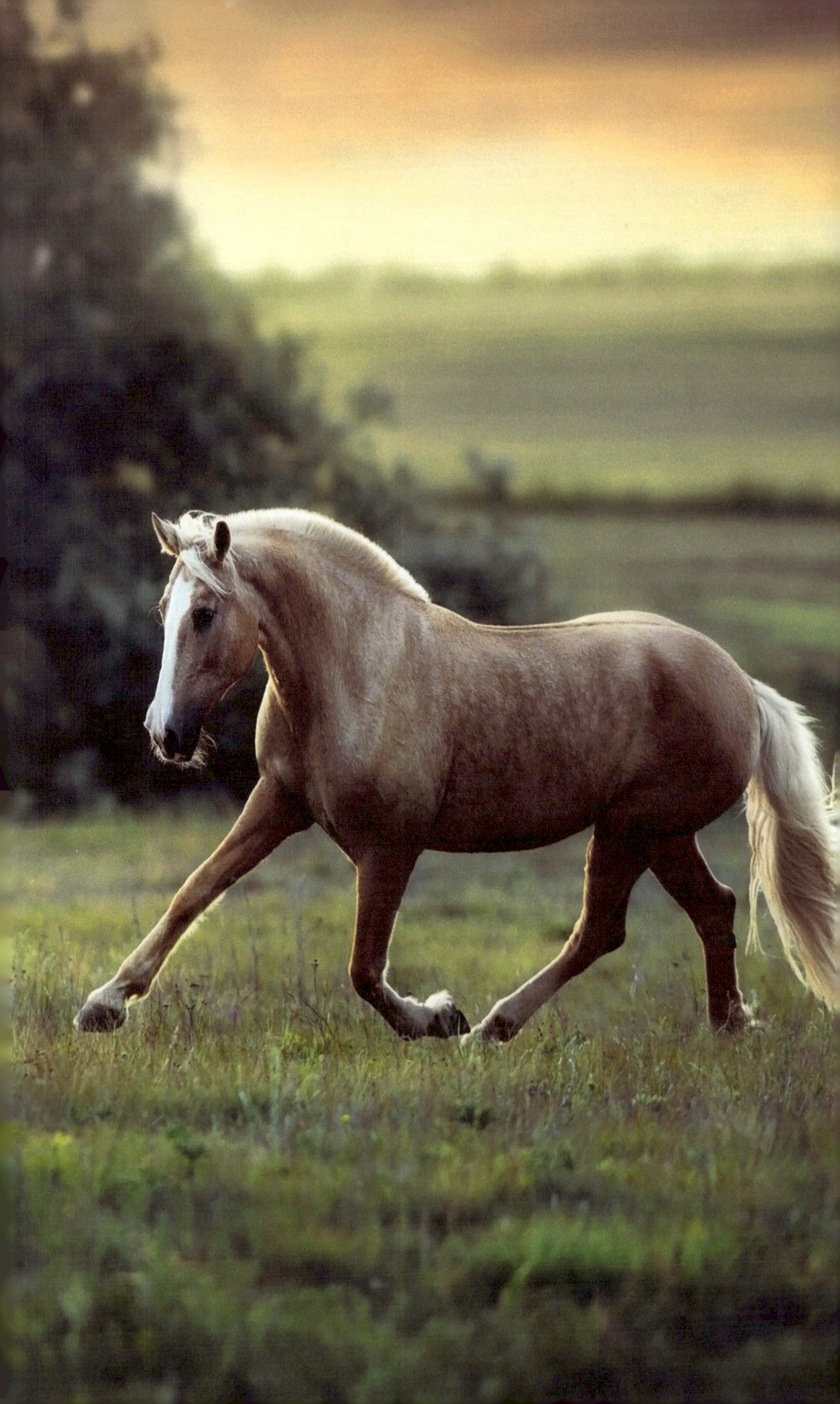

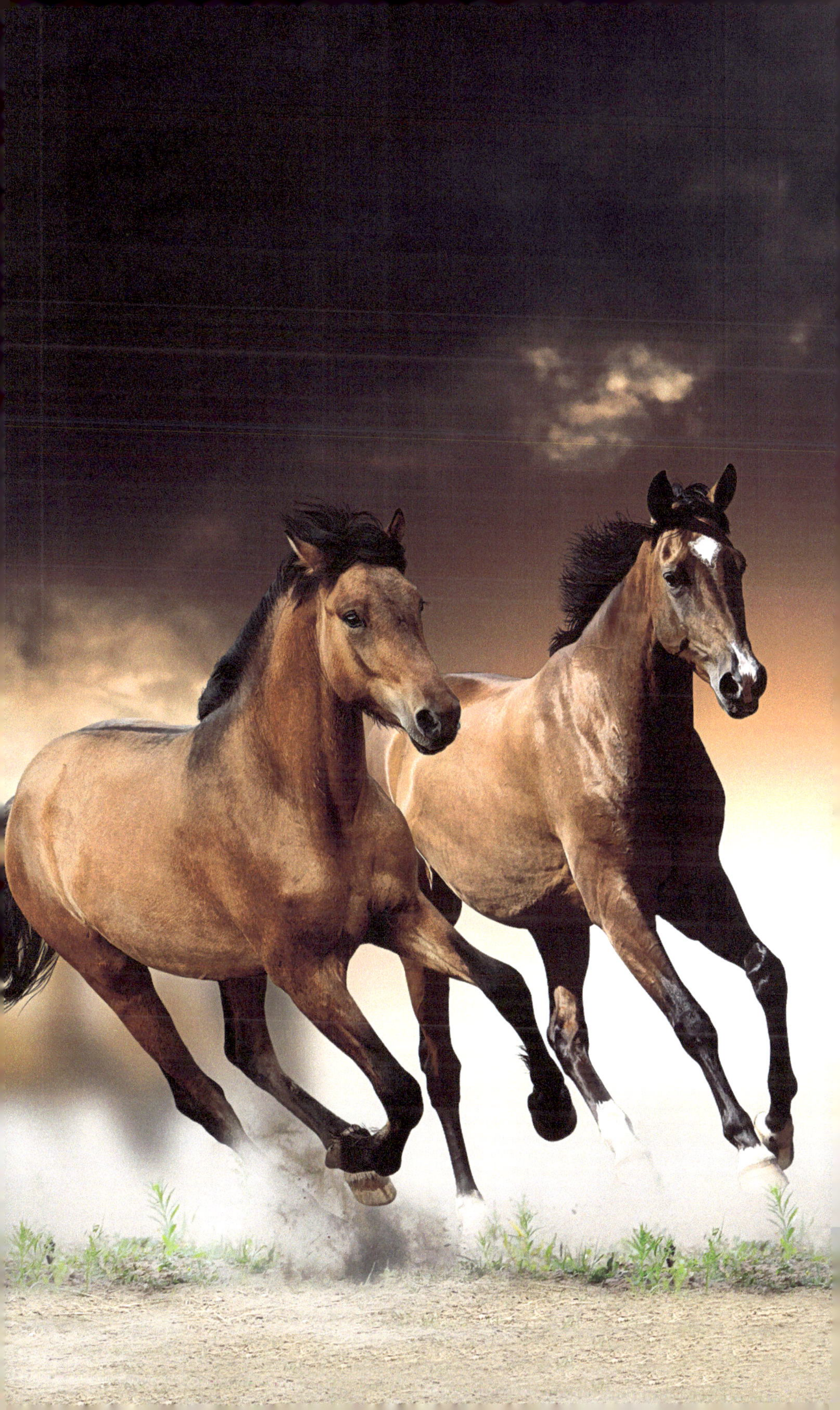

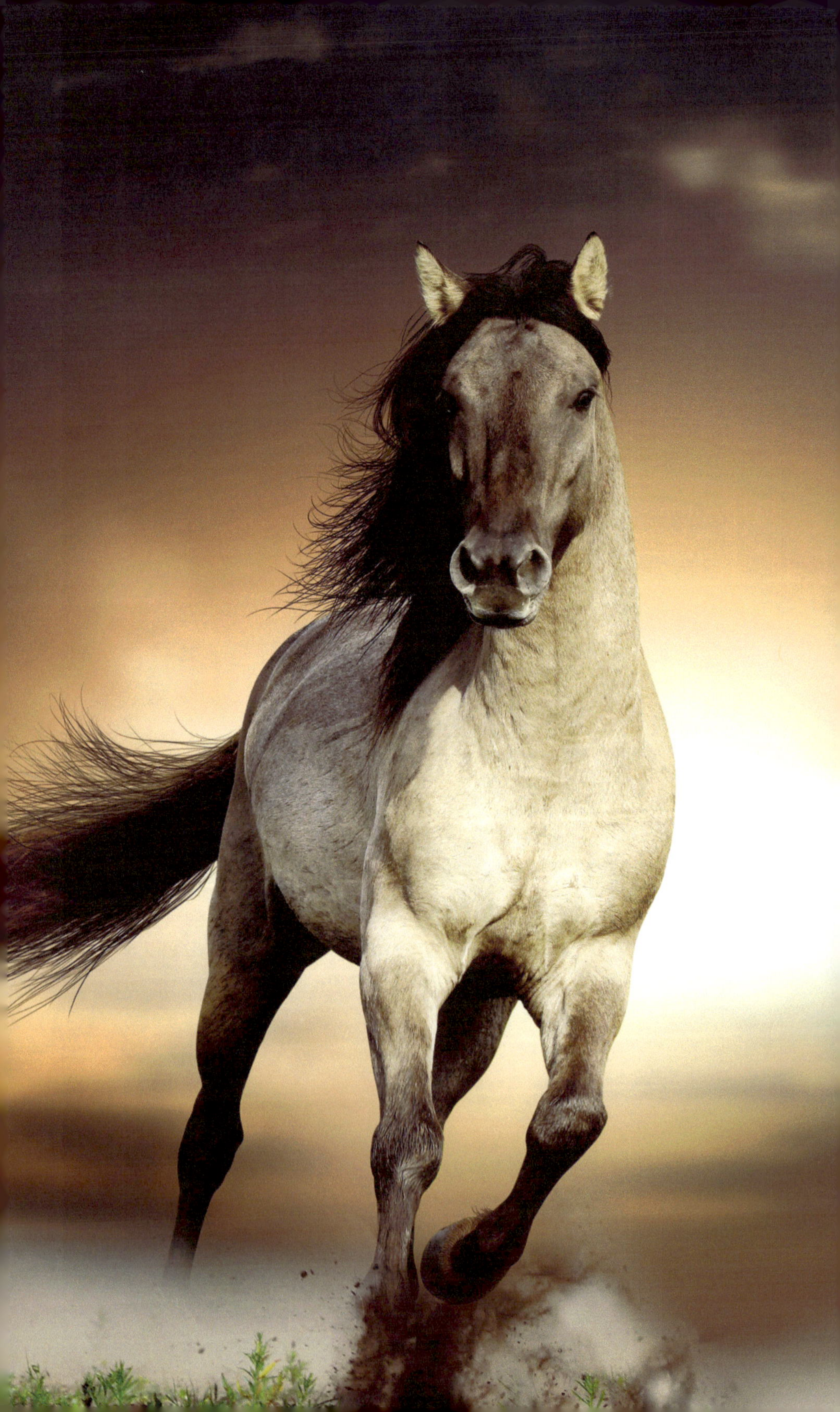

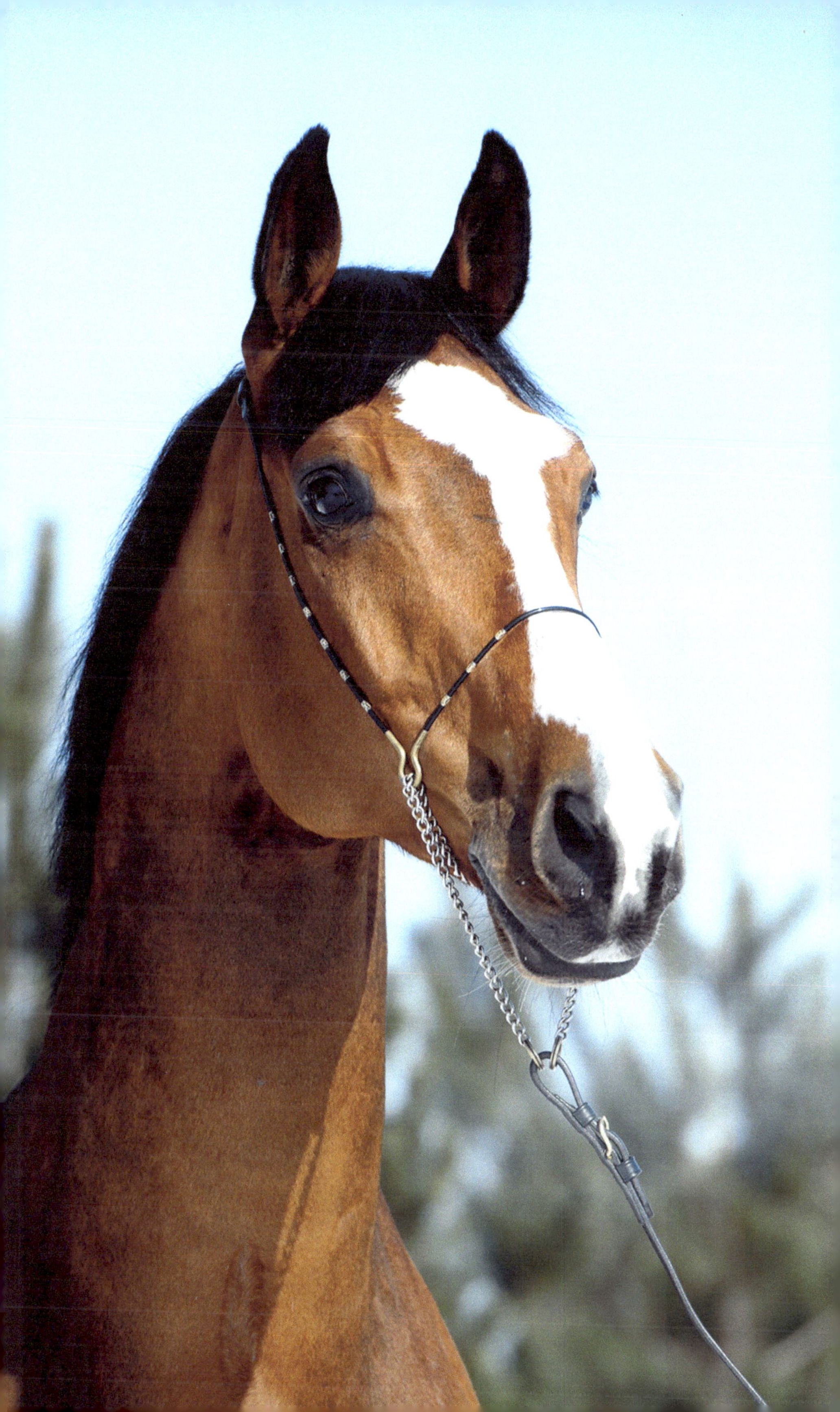

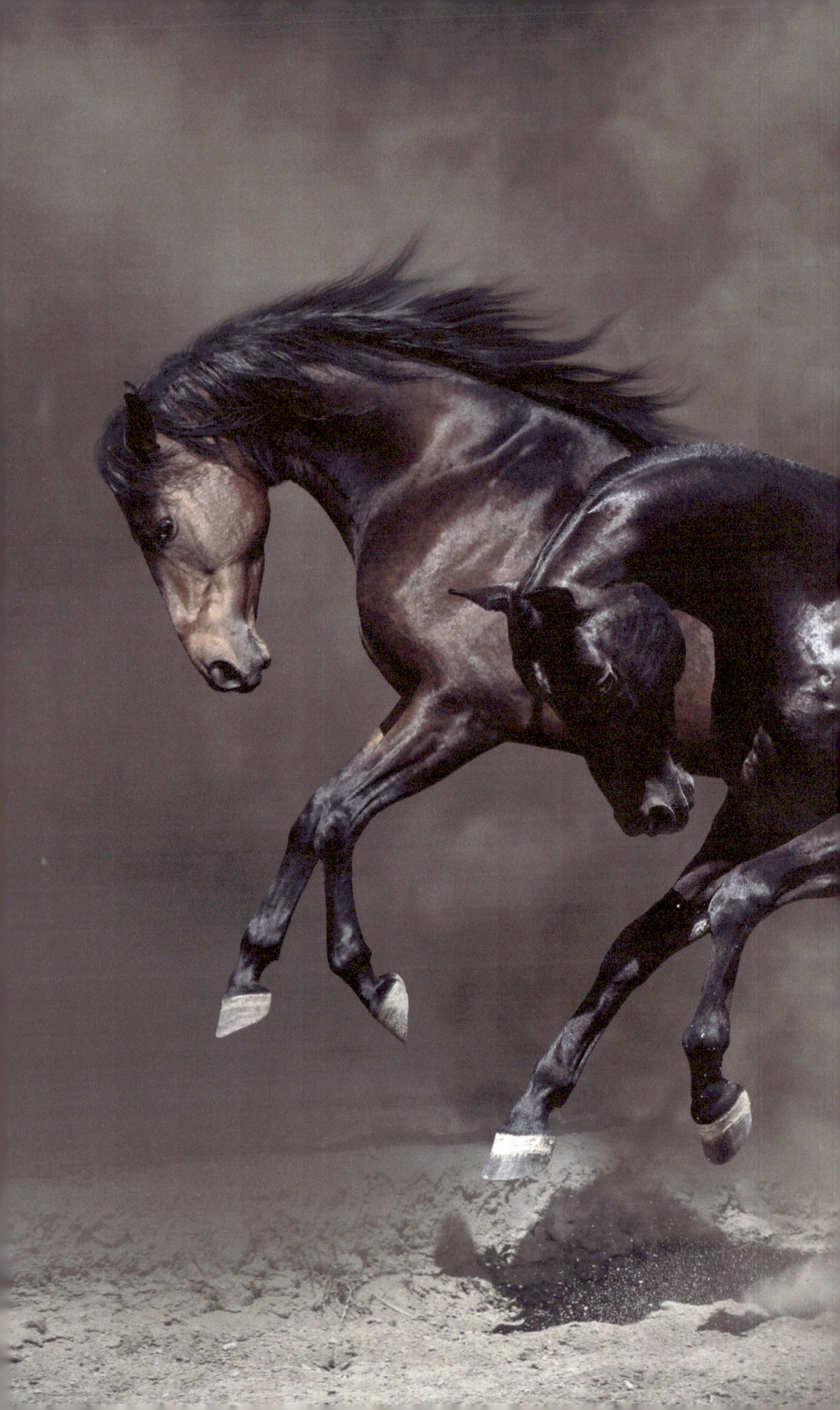

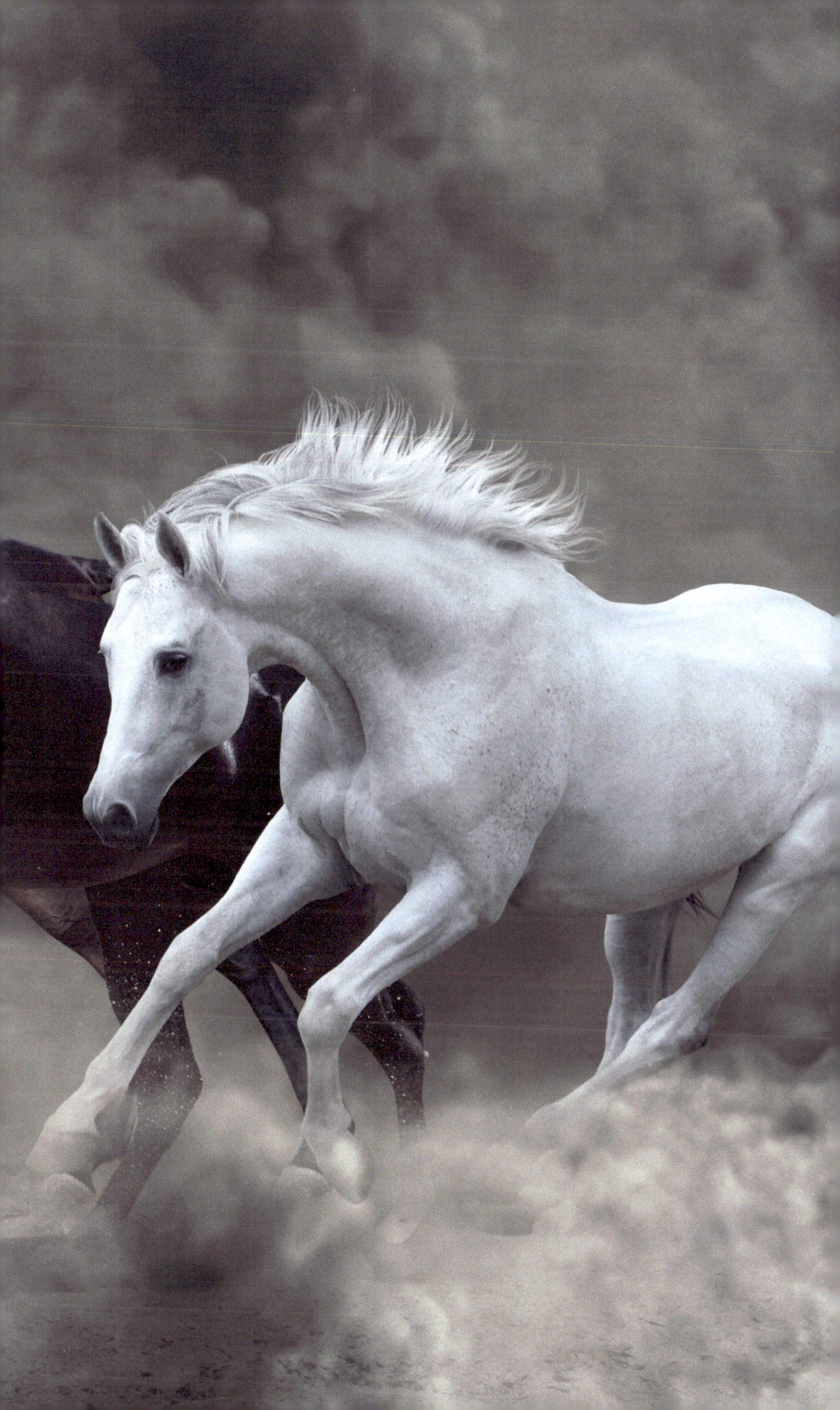

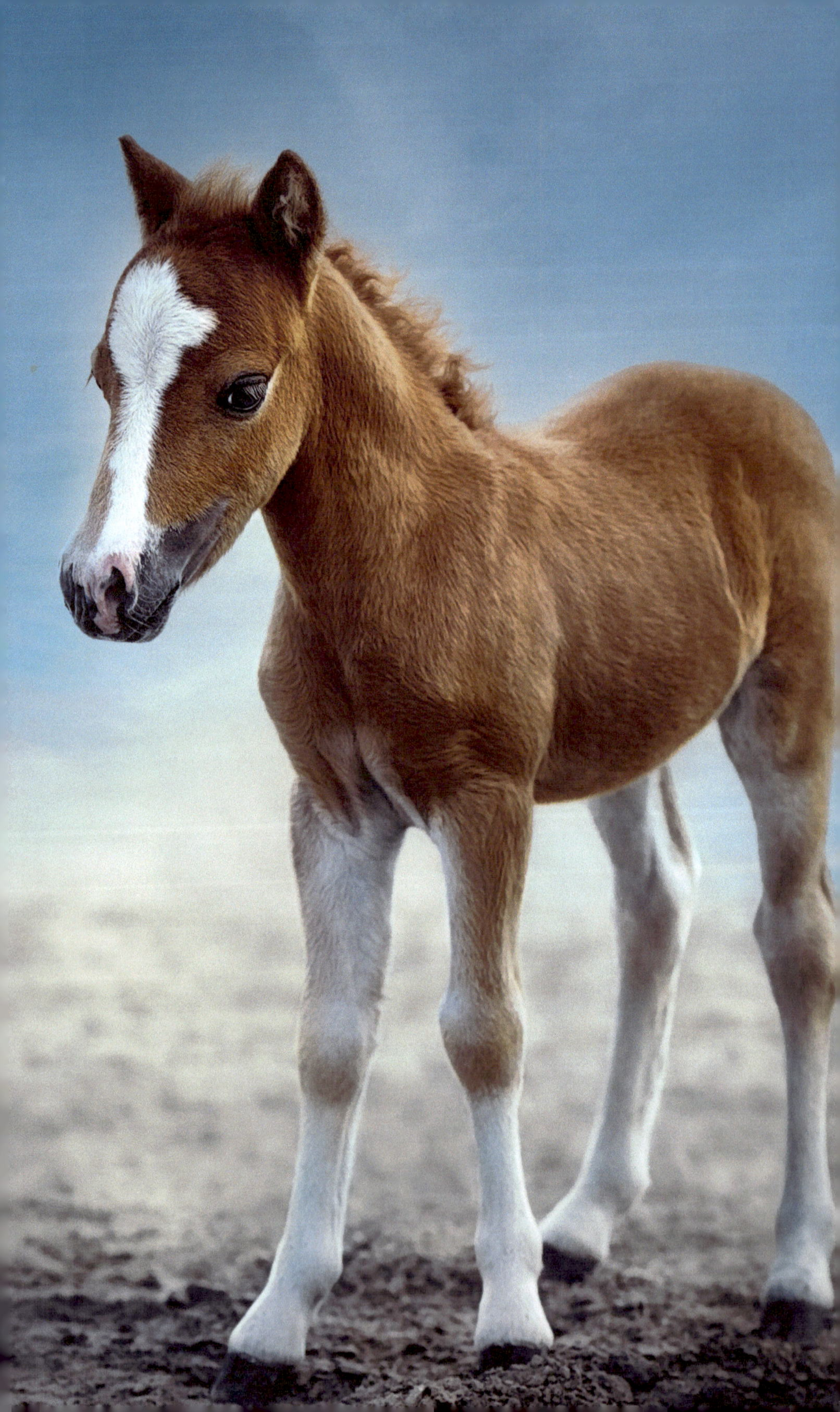

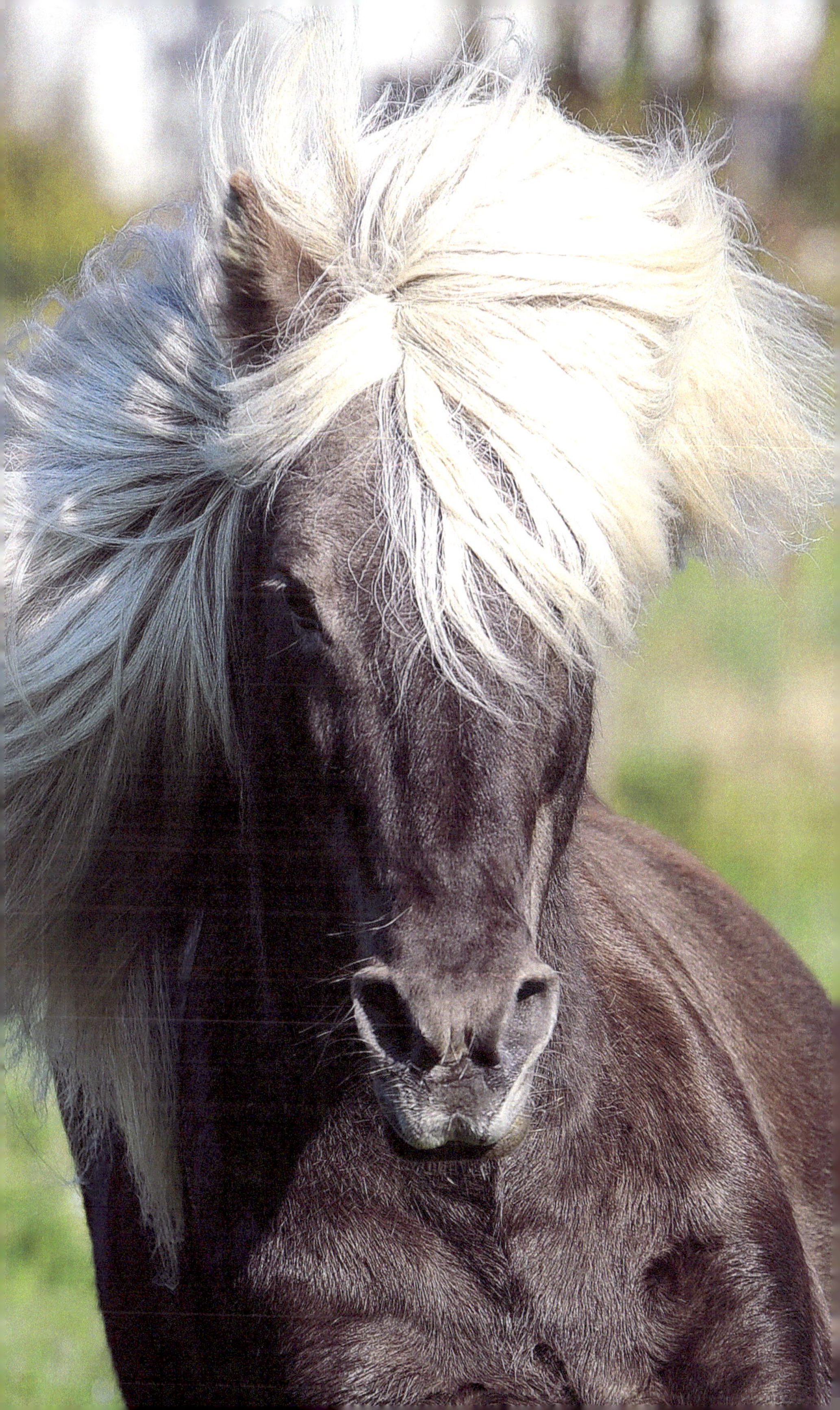

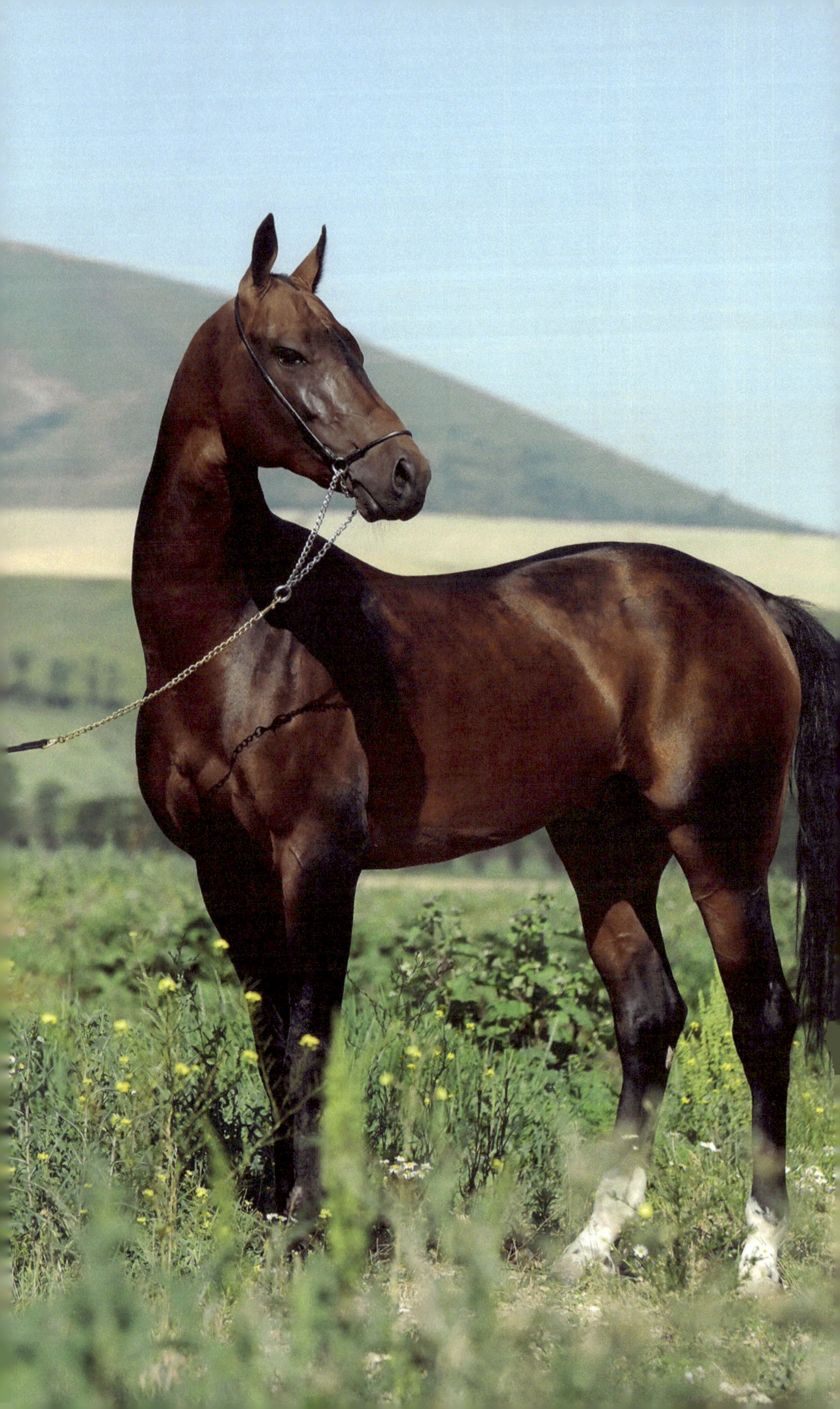

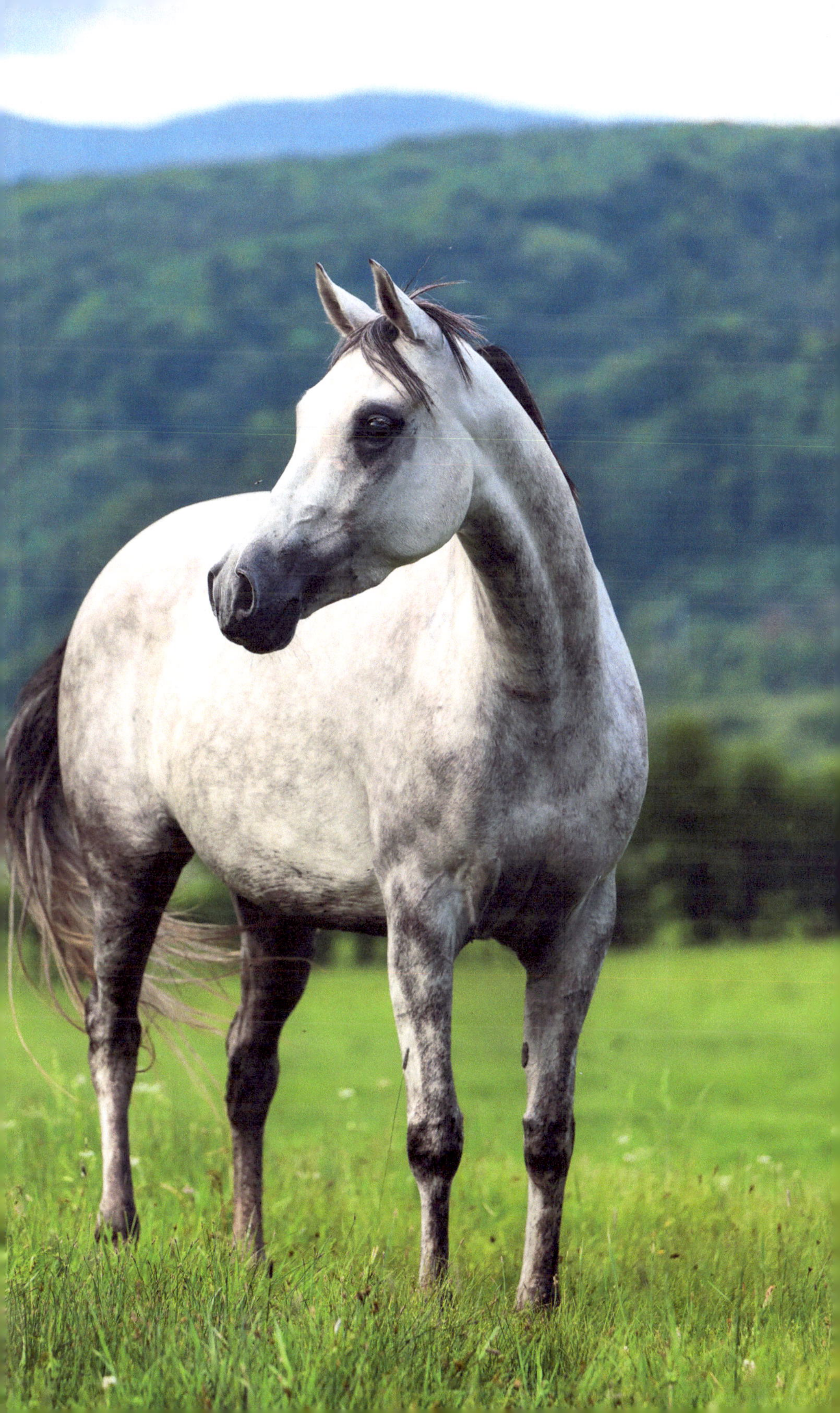

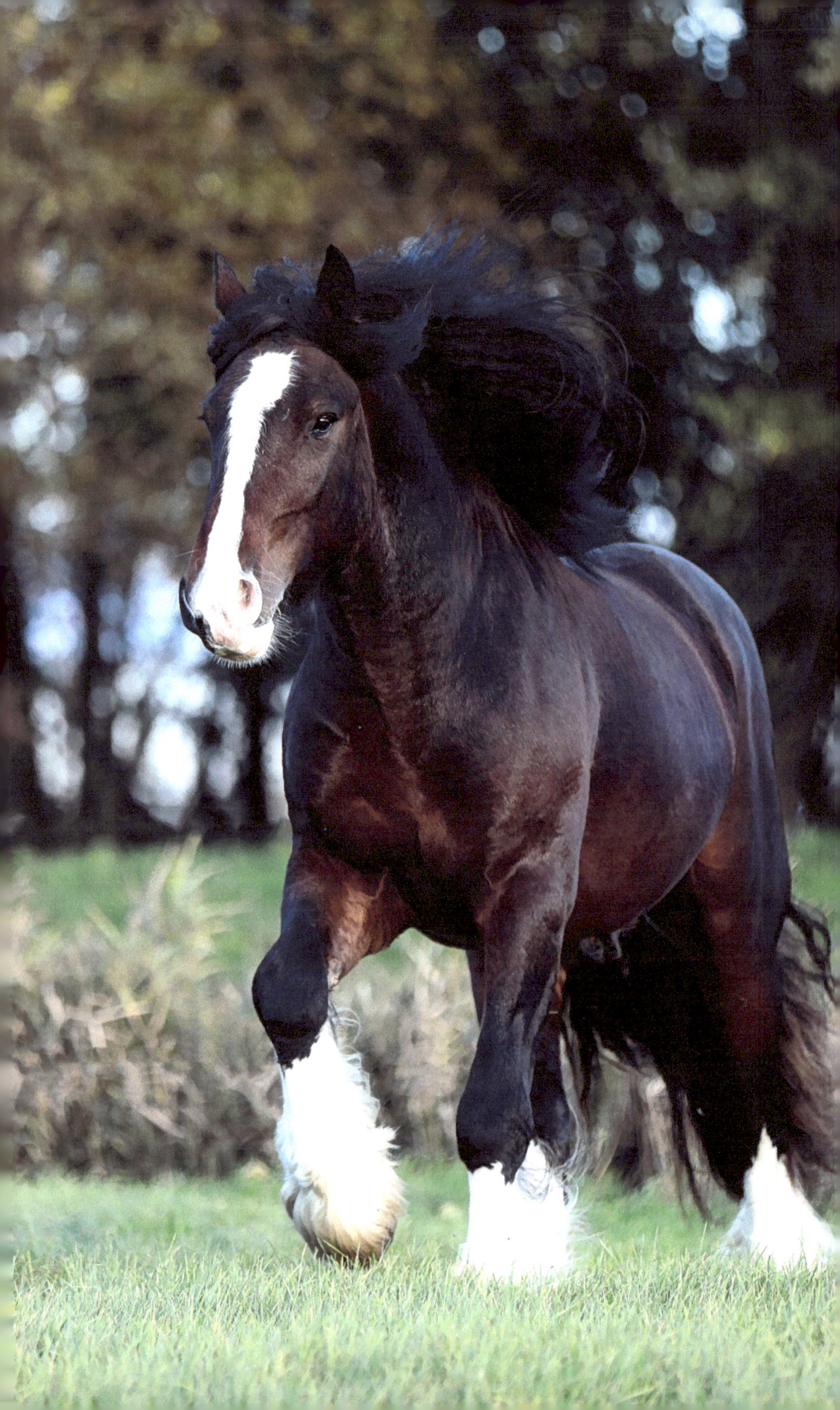

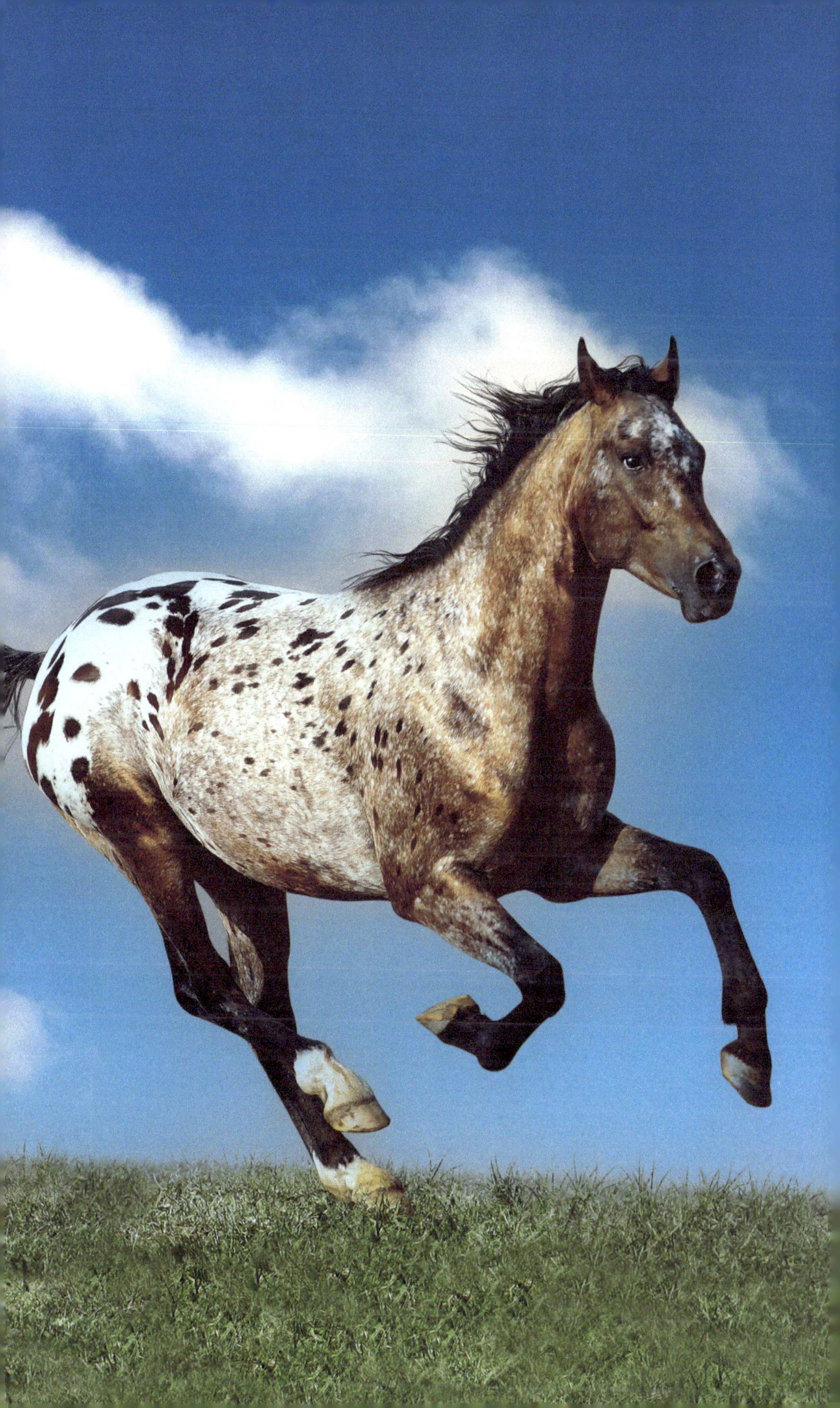

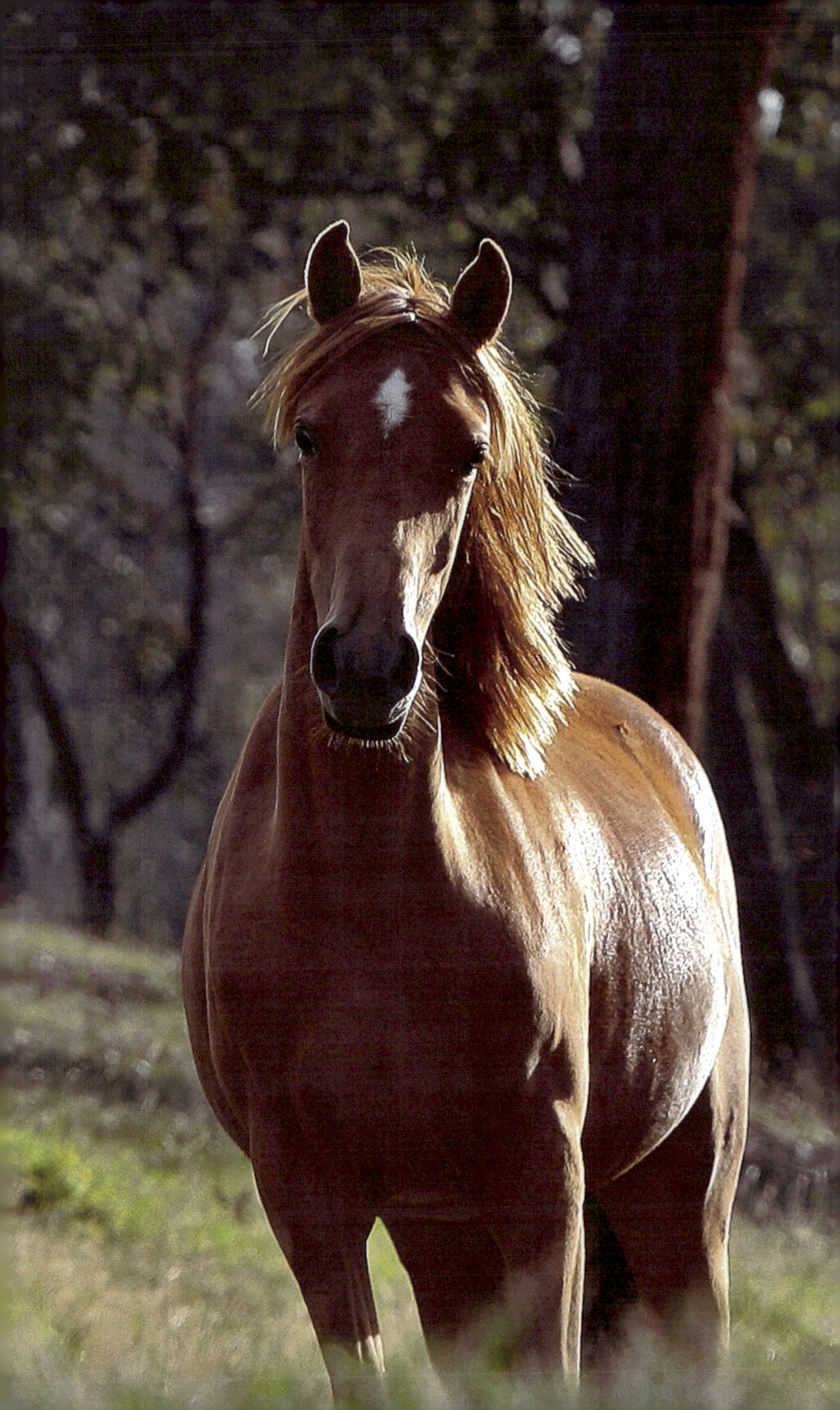

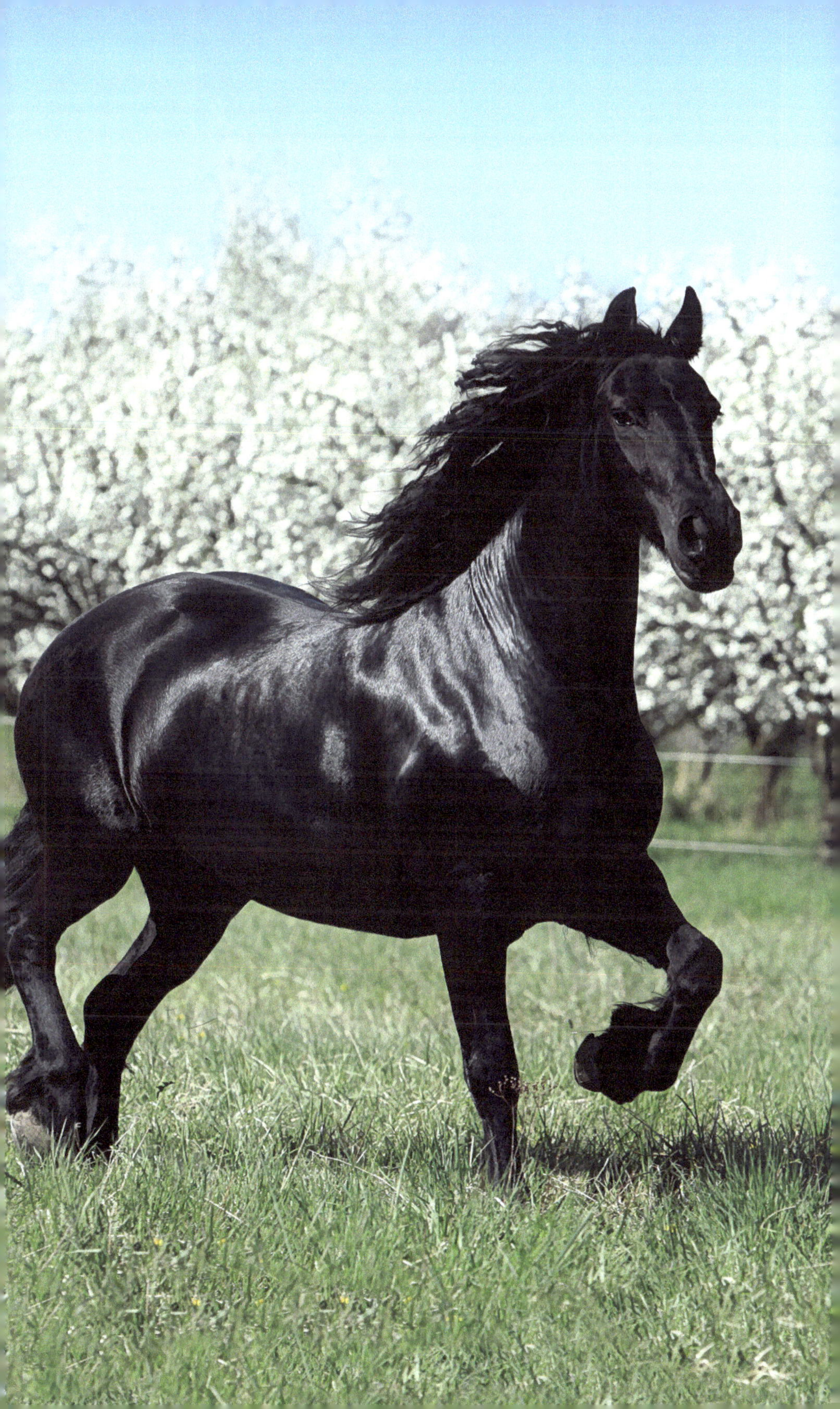